r o b   f r o s t

living
waters

for your

parched
prayers

Chariot Victor Publishing
A Division of Cook Communications

Chariot Victor Publishing
Cook Communications, Colorado Springs, CO 80918
Cook Communications, Paris, Ontario
Kingsway Communications, Eastbourne, England

LIVING WATERS FOR YOUR PARCHED PRAYERS
This edition issued by special arrangement with
Kingsway Publications, Lottbridge Drove, Eastbourne,
East Sussex, England, BN23 6NT.

First U.S. edition 1999
Printed in the United States of America.

Design: Image Studios

1 2 3 4 5 6 7 8 9 10 Printing/Year 03 02 01 00 99

Library of Congress Cataloging-in-Publication Data
Frost, Rob
            Living waters for your parched prayers/Rob Frost.--1st U.S.
ed.
            p.   cm.
     ISBN 1-56476-712-4
            1. Prayer--Christianity.   I. Title.
BV215.F766   1999   98-48290
248.3'2--dc21   CIP

Bible quotations are taken from the *Good News Bible* © American Bible Society 1976,
published by the Bible Societies and Collins. Use is made of the King James Version
(KJV), *The Living Bible* (TLB), © 1971, Tyndale House Publishers, Wheaton, IL 60189.
Used by permission; *Holy Bible: New International Version*®. Copyright © 1973, 1978,
1984 by International Bible Society. Used by permission of Zondervan Publishing
House. All rights reserved. Scripture quotations used at the end of each chapter are
taken from *The Message*. Copyright © 1993. Used by permission of NavPress
Publishing House.

....

To Jacqui, my lifelong prayer partner

....

contents

acknowledgments

My thanks to all those who have encouraged me in the life of prayer, and particularly to Clive Jones, my prayer partner for fourteen years, and all who prayerfully support me in my work.

Particular thanks to Meryl Smith for typing endless pages of illegible manuscript and to Richard Smith for scanning the material with his usual eye for detail!

introduction

Many people find prayer difficult, and the very thought of getting into prayer seems off-putting.

In this personal view of the life of prayer I will be sharing insights for daily devotions. This is not an in-depth study guide or manual about prayer; it's a sharing from one heart to another. It is a book for anyone who feels a failure at prayer and who would welcome some encouragement in the struggle. For the one whose prayer life feels parched—searching for the living waters of a vital relationship with God.

Some of this material has appeared in a different form in magazine articles, sermons and books. The poems and meditations are thoughts which I have written over the years or gleaned from treasured devotional books. The biblical passages are taken from *The Message* paraphrase, which brings the Gospel message home in a refreshingly different way. I hope that this material will be brought out again and again when familiar struggles with prayer return.

Rob Frost

ONE

when I don't feel like praying

When I was a Sea Scout (complete with short trousers and sailor hat!) our troop rented an old Thames sailing cutter for a cruise across the English Channel. It was a fascinating experience discovering how to rely on the wind and the tide to get us to the right place at the right time!

Returning back across the Channel from Belgium, we hit a terrible storm which lasted for twenty-four hours. I've never been so scared—or so seasick—in my life! The deck was like a skating rink, and sheets of sea spray crashed over us every few seconds.

In order to trim the sails and move about on deck, we were each issued a safety harness. We were able to move around by clipping and reclipping the harness onto safety rails across the deck. The power of the waves was tremendous, and at any moment I felt I might be swept overboard.

As the storm continued I became more and more reliant on that safety harness. My life depended on it. Even when the water hit me I could lean back and feel it taking my weight. I developed a strong sense of trust in that short piece of wire!

My relationship with Jesus has developed in much the same way. Through all life's joys and sorrows I've learned to put my weight on Jesus, and to discover that He's the kind of friend who is always there, no matter how I feel.

Some years ago, I met an old African-American preacher from the United States who spoke about "faith" and "feelings." "Sometimes I feel high," he said, "and sometimes I feel low. I never go along in a straight line!" Most of us are just the same—our feelings vary with each new day and with each new situation.

I must admit that sometimes Jesus doesn't feel close to me. But my relationship with Him doesn't rest on feelings; it rests on facts. It's not feelings that drive me to seek His presence . . . it's my commitment to Him. When I don't feel like praying I know deep down that He is still with me—even then!

Because I am committed to Him I force myself to meet Him, and struggle to make space to share my life with Him. Feelings come and go, and I don't measure my relationship with Jesus by them. I rest on facts. The fact that He has died for me, and the fact that I have received Him into my life as Lord and Savior.

My relationship with Jesus is a "good days/bad days" kind of relationship. We share the kind of friendship that grows even stronger in the difficult times. There is a stability about my love for Him and His love for me which is the foundation of who I am. I cannot gauge my prayer life by feelings. They are a dangerous and unreliable indicator. Even when I don't feel like praying I know that He understands me.

My experience of Jesus doesn't depend on a series of emotional highs and lows. It isn't about leaping from one great spiritual "fix" to another. It is about struggling to talk to Him, and making myself available to Him when prayer is the last thing on my mind.

If I'm honest, I think my friendship with Jesus has grown most in the difficult times. My greatest glimpses of His love have come when I've been really down and haven't known where to turn, except to Him. My commitment to Jesus is the basis of everything, and it's a commitment that brings me back to Him when I'd really rather turn away.

When people try to give the impression that they're good at prayer, I'm immediately suspicious. I certainly don't make such a claim for myself. For me, at least, prayer is a struggle, and it always has been.

I believe there is a lot of hypocrisy about prayer in the church. People make out that they've found the best way of praying, or that there is some formula for making prayer easy. Lots of Christians also feel guilty about prayer. They are afraid to tell others just how much of a struggle their prayer life really is, and how they have never felt much good at it.

If this book encourages anyone who is struggling with the life of prayer, then it will have fulfilled its purpose. In the following pages I'll be sharing some of the reticence with which I approach prayer, and some of the thoughts and convictions which keep me going when I would rather give up.

I am sure that there are as many ways of prayer as there are Christians. You'll find no simple formulas or easy guides to prayer here, just the confessions of someone who feels rather pathetic at prayer and who wants to encourage others who feel just as hopeless!

For me, the bottom line is not about how we pray, but about how we keep up the struggle, how we press on with the journey, and how we keep trying at prayer. For in the end, prayer is a relationship, and like all relationships it has to be worked at, day in and day out.

Today, remember that Jesus is with you. His presence does not rest on how you feel . . . it rests on His promises. Pause and remember His presence with you, and then, in silence, put your weight on Him, and Him alone, for He is your safety harness when the strong storms blow.

Live in me. Make your home in me just as I do in you. In the same way that a branch can't bear grapes by itself but only by being joined to the vine, you can't bear fruit unless you are joined with me.

I am the Vine, you are the branches. When you're joined with me and I with you, the relation intimate and organic, the harvest is sure to be abundant. Separated, you can't produce a thing. Anyone who separates from me is deadwood, gathered up and thrown on the bonfire. But if you make yourselves at home with me and my words are at home in you, you can be sure that whatever you ask will be listened to and acted upon.

John 15: 4-7

Lord, I feel fed up today
And I don't really want to pray.

Things are hard for me today
And I'm too depressed to care.

I guess I'm tired and drained
    I've done so much,
    been through so much,
    With nothing more to give.

Lord I come to you:
    In laziness,
    Half-heartedness
    And apathetic disbelief

And I praise you:
    With my mind,
    though my emotions aren't engaged;
    With my lips,
    though my heart is cold;
    With my will,
    though my spirit seems so dead.

Pour Your love afresh into my life, I pray,
And accept me
In my weariness.

T W O

when I've lost my way

My family knows that I'm always losing things—my car keys, my diary, and even my checkbook! Whenever I cry, "Has anyone seen my. . .?" my wife replies, "When did you last see it?" I must retrace my steps and go back to when I last saw it.

At times when my mission has been going wrong, when the work has been difficult, the results negligible or when I feel I've failed . . . I know there's only one way ahead: I must retrace my steps to the One who sent me.

One morning, I walked past Whitby Abbey and down the hundred and ninety-nine steps to the old town below. Everything was still—it was too early for the tourists! The narrow streets were empty and deserted save for the clatter of a distant milk truck. I paused to look in the tiny shop windows. I was in no hurry; the morning was mine.

I ambled down the cobbled streets; it felt good to be alive. As I crossed the harbor bridge I paused to look out to sea. In the distance there was a line of small fishing boats chugging out of the morning mist toward me. Seagulls wheeled above them, hoping for a share of the catch. It was a beautiful sight.

It was one of those timeless mornings: no pressure, no rush, no impending deadlines. The air of calm and stillness enveloped me. I was aware that Jesus was with me. I drank in the sights and sounds of that peaceful morning scene, and praised Him for His goodness.

Within a few minutes the boats were moored alongside the quay and the fish market was a hive of activity. A squeaky crane was hauling crates of dripping fish from the decks of the laden boats, and there was a noisy babble of conversation all around.

I saw a larger boat moored beside the quay. As I moved closer I noticed a group of fishermen bending low over their nets. Slowly they dragged the huge trawl-net across the deck. Whenever they found a tear they took some orange twine and repaired it. As I stood and watched, my mind raced back to another group of fishermen by the waterside long ago.

"Peter, do you love Me?"

There were a hundred and one things which Jesus could have talked about. There was the work of evangelism, the mission of the church, and the future of the kingdom for a start! But Jesus knew that He only had to get one thing straight.

Love had to be the starting point. Peter had to get this sorted before the breathtaking story of Acts could unfold. If this was right then everything else would fall into place.

But what a question! Hadn't Peter given enough by leaving everything behind to follow Jesus? Hadn't he risked enough by staking his reputation on a wandering teacher? Hadn't he done enough, this Peter the rock, on whom the church would be built?

No. Peter's denial before the cockcrow had to be faced. His unfaithfulness had to be dealt with. All the sacrifices and all the good deeds didn't mean anything unless he could look Jesus in the eye and say, "I love You."

"Peter, do you love Me more than these?"

The boat, the fish, the tackle. The business, the livelihood, the culture of the Galilean fisherman. The camaraderie of the crew, the good times on the lake. The family, the friends, the faithful crew. The safe, ordered life passed on down the generations of Galilean fishermen. Did he really love Jesus more than these?

Peter's love for Jesus couldn't be a divided love. It had to be a love which outweighed every human consideration; a love which Jesus warned might demand the ultimate sacrifice . . . a love without compromise.

Three times the question came; three times the answer given—without hesitation, confident, assured. And so the work could begin: "Feed My sheep."

This is the love which lies at the heart of the Christian life. Christian lifestyle begins with a self-denial relationship which declares, "Jesus, I love You."

Today, retrace your steps to Jesus. Past all the complex difficulties and dilemmas of your life. Past all the broken promises and ruins of your discipleship. Past all the failures of the years. Go back to Jesus, and tell Him that you love Him.

I ask him to strengthen you by his Spirit—not a brute strength but a glorious inner strength—that Christ will live in you as you open the door and invite him in. And I ask him that with both feet planted firmly on love, you'll be able to take in with all Christians the extravagant dimensions of Christ's love. Reach out and experience the breadth! Test its length! Plumb the depths! Rise to the heights! Live full lives, full in the fullness of God.

God can do anything, you know—far more than you could ever imagine or request in your wildest dreams! He does it not by pushing us around but by working within us, his Spirit deeply and gently within us.

Ephesians 3:16-20

"Grant me, O most loving Lord, to rest in Thee . . . For surely my heart cannot truly find rest, nor be entirely contented, unless it rest in Thee. Amen."

Thomas à Kempis (1379-1471)

O Lord our God,
grant us grace
to desire Thee
with our whole heart;
that so desiring
we may seek and find Thee;
and so finding Thee
may love Thee;
and loving Thee,
may hate those sins from which
Thou hast redeemed us.
Amen.

Anselm (1033-1109)

THREE

when I've grown self-centered

I remember it as if it were yesterday. I parked the car in the hospital parking lot and helped my pregnant wife out of the passenger seat. We walked up the stone steps and into the reception area. It was after midnight and our footsteps echoed around the empty hallway. We stepped toward the door marked "Maternity" and went through.

It was a long tunnel-like corridor, and tubular lights cast a harsh, unfriendly glare along the green walls. There was a strong smell of disinfectant, and somewhere in the distance doors banged and trolleys rattled. I heard the whisper of hushed voices behind closed doors.

My wife, who was about to give birth to our first child, hobbled slowly along. I did my best to support her. The walk seemed endless. At last we reached a large green door and arrived at the maternity suite. A team of smartly dressed nurses hovered around us. They spoke to each other in short clipped phrases and gave us reassuring smiles.

The machinery shocked me. After all, we had come for the birth of a baby, not the servicing of a motor vehicle! Needles flickered, lights flashed . . . and the room echoed with the amplified beat of the unborn baby's heart. Then the sound of the heartbeat changed, an alarm sounded . . . and the room was filled with masked figures speaking orders in medical terminology. We were in the twilight zone between life and death.

Suddenly with a scream and a gasp the baby was born. A boy! And there, unbelievably, nestling in my arms was my newborn son. So vulnerable. So delicate. So fragile. A tiny bundle of wriggling humanity. I held his tiny hand in mine.

The faceless team left us, and we were alone. My wife and I looked at each other and at our son, and marveled at God's gift of new life. We thanked the Lord for him. It was a precious moment, and one which I will remember forever.

A few months later, I parked my car again in the same parking lot, climbed the same stone steps and walked through the empty hallway. Again it was well after midnight. I stepped into the large rattling elevator and went up to the fourth floor. The creaking doors rolled apart and I walked down the corridor toward the ward.

I opened the doors and looked inside. Everything was quiet in the darkened ward. The dim night light revealed a long row of beds on either side. There was an air of stillness. The patients were all asleep. The nurse looked up from her desk and came to greet me.

She led me into a small anteroom. I was dazzled by the harsh fluorescent lighting. And then I saw her—unconscious. Her head propped up on pillows. Her husband was sitting on the bed beside her, holding her hand. He looked gray and weary. He gave a glance of recognition.

We sat, hour after hour, holding her hands. Occasionally we exchanged words and glances—as if in reassurance. The patient lay still, save for the shallow, labored breathing. We prayed aloud and read Psalm 23. I silently offered the whole situation to the Lord and confessed my own inadequacy to share in it. The breathing worsened, becoming more labored and more difficult. I felt a tingling pang of fear as I sensed that death was near.

Then, without any drama or struggle, the breathing stopped. There was an intensity of silence. She was dead . . . and we were left holding her hands and feeling awkward. I prayed, and committed her to the Lord, then I walked her husband back toward the elevator. The wonder of life and death and the pain of good-byes filled my mind.

Those two nights in the hospital became closely associated in my thinking. I had held the tiny hand of my newborn son, and I had held the hand of a dying friend. I had shared in the mystery of life and death.

In the emptiness of the baby's hand and the emptiness of the dying lady's hand, I saw the stupidity of so much of my own earthly struggle. I saw again the futility of my own desire to possess, to make my mark, or to get ahead.

I am mortal, God is immortal. I am temporal, He is eternal. I am finite, He is infinite. I am nothing, He is everything. I am human, He is God!

Prayer takes us beyond the sphere of our knowing; beyond our material universe and into another dimension. Prayer is our approach to One who is superior, pre-eminent, matchless and incomparable.

Prayer is a moment to touch the eternal, to glimpse the holy, to be enfolded in perfect Love. Prayer is moving beyond the confines of my own self-centeredness to meet the One who created me for so much more.

Today, reach out beyond yourself to Jesus. For in finding Him, you will find yourself.

We look at this Son and see the God who cannot be seen. We look at this Son and see God's original purpose in everything created. For everything, absolutely everything, above and below, visible and invisible, rank after rank after rank of angels—everything got started in him and finds its purpose in him. He was there before any of it came into existence and holds it all together right up to this moment. And when it comes to the church, he organizes and holds it together, like a head does a body.

He was supreme in the beginning and—leading the resurrection parade—he is supreme in the end. From beginning to end he's there, towering far above everything, everyone. So spacious is he, so roomy, that everything of God finds its proper place in him without crowding. Not only that, but all the broken and dislocated pieces of the universe—people and things, animals and atoms—get properly fixed and fit together in vibrant harmonies, all because of his death, his blood that poured down from the Cross.

Colossians 1:15-20

Look up! Look up at the sky!
Who created all those stars you see?
The One who leads them out like an army.
He knows how many there are.
He calls each one by name.
His power is so great, not one is ever missing!

Look up at the sky!
Stop putting yourself at the center of your
    world.
See the greatness of God
And you'll see everything in true perspective.

Look up at the sky!
Lift your heart above the synthetic
And glimpse One so much greater.

His glory is reflected in the changing sky
His greatness and majesty are beyond
    compare!
He made the universe
and all that's in it.
His power can't be measured
Nor His glory imagined.

Look up at the sky!
To whom can the holy God be compared?

F O U R

when I'm stressed

My whole body had become a tense, nervous knot. In only a matter of weeks it seemed that I'd forgotten how to relax and even how to laugh. I'd seen these symptoms in the lives of others, but never so obviously in my own.

I knew that I needed to take note of some of the advice I'd given to others and to tackle the stress that was tensing me up. My wife didn't so much suggest that we take a vacation as insist upon it! We saw an ad for "Bargains in Greece" and twelve hours later we were on a plane bound for the tiny island of Lesbos.

Early on in the vacation we took a trip across the bay to Turkey, and to the ancient city of Pergamum. The guide took us to what she declared was "the oldest hospital in the world." It was fascinating to walk along pathways where patients took the air more than 2,000 years ago. As I walked beside the ruined wards I felt mysteriously connected to the past.

The guide explained that much of the treatment was aimed at stress-related illnesses, and that the therapy was designed to help the ancient Greeks relax. Mud baths, role play, exercise, and entertainment were all used to help them unwind! It was strange to think that such radical treatments were used so long ago!

The next day I sat alone on the small terrace and allowed the tranquillity of the scene to wash over me. I gazed across at the beautiful blue bay, the gently sloping olive groves, and the misty azure sky. And all around was the distant whir of crickets.

I opened my Bible and read Luke 12. They were words that I knew well and had often expounded upon, but there was a new power in them that day. I felt that Jesus had spoken them just for me.

Jesus was talking to people under stress. He told them that He would be crucified and that they would be persecuted . . . and, naturally, they were worried! They wondered how they would defend themselves against synagogues and governors, and how they'd cope with persecution and humiliation. He was addressing real people with real problems—people who knew sleepless nights, worries about the future, and the fear of the unknown. He was also speaking to me.

"Look how the wildflowers grow," he said. "They don't work or make clothes for themselves. But I tell you that not even King Solomon with all his wealth had clothes as beautiful as one of these flowers."

I certainly didn't feel like a wildflower! As I looked back across my hectic schedule of the previous weeks and remembered the strain and sleepless nights, I saw myself more as a dried-up weed!

From this faraway place I looked back at the hectic lifestyle that I'd been trapped in and saw more clearly just how empty much of it really was. Now that I was away from my daily round of meetings and appointments I could see things from a different perspective.

I sat on the terrace outside the apartment and gazed at the clusters of bright red poppies in among the olive groves. They glowed with color in the spring sunshine. They weren't struggling and straining, muttering or complaining—they just bloomed!

"Look how the wildflowers grow." They just absorb the light, the dew and the warmth—and they bloom. I needed to spend time alone with the Lord and to absorb more of the light and warmth of His presence.

There and then I bathed in the radiance and love of Christ. I glimpsed the vastness of His love. I felt enfolded. I recognized again that there was no part of me outside His knowledge or His care. There was no aspect of my life He didn't understand and no insecurity of which He was unaware. The boundless love of the Lord flooded over me like a healing stream, releasing tension and care. I felt my whole being renewed and made whole again.

The words of Maclaren summed it up: "Whoever is able to say to himself, 'I am,' will never know rest until he can turn to God and say, 'Thou art,' and then, laying his hand in the great Father's hand, venture to say, 'We are.'"

Perhaps you are worn down by worry. Maybe you're stressed by responsibilities at home or work, or concerned about your health or future. Take time out, turn to Jesus,

and receive from Him that stream of renewing power
which can release you from your stress and give you peace.

*Walk into the fields and look at the wildflowers. They don't
fuss with their appearance—but have you ever seen color and
design quite like it? The ten best-dressed men and women in
the country look shabby alongside them. If God gives such
attention to the wildflowers, most of them never even seen,
don't you think he'll attend to you, take pride in you, do his
best for you?*

*What I'm trying to do here is get you to relax, not be so
preoccupied with getting, so you can respond to God's giving.
People who don't know God and the way he works fuss over
these things, but you know both God and how he works. Steep
yourself in God-reality, God-initiative, God-provisions. You'll
find all your everyday human concerns will be met. Don't be
afraid of missing out. You're my dearest friends! The Father
wants to give you the very kingdom itself.*

Luke 12:27-32

In the tension of these moments
Will You come to me, my Lord?
Share Your presence, share Your goodness,
God on whom I do depend?

Come, my Savior, walk beside me
through the schedule of my day,
meet me in my many meetings,
guide me when I pause to pray.

Lord I know that You are with me
in this quickly passing day.
Help me not to miss Your coming,
do not let me turn away.

Lord I met You in the good times,
when my way ahead seemed sure.
Now, please come and walk beside me,
and stay close for evermore.

FIVE

when I think that I know best

Sometimes, when I think that I know best, I think about the potter and the clay. In my heart I know that I can only discover the purpose of my being, only reach my full potential, and only become what God intended, when I offer myself like clay in His hands.

When I was a child we used to go on vacation to a small Cotswold village called Hook Norton. On one occasion my cousins and I went out into a field and found a marshy pool and a grassy bank of damp clay soil.

I enjoyed stripping away the grass and digging out the clay with my bare hands. We hacked out great lumps of it and wrapped it in newspaper, then we proudly carried it back to the farm and put it on the kitchen table!

There, in the farmyard kitchen, my aunt encouraged

us to make simple shapes out of it. Later on she "fired" them in the old coke oven, and then, when they were hard, we painted them. It amazed me how the clay had changed between the field and the mantelpiece!

Years later, as a married man, I was Christmas shopping with my family in London's busy Oxford Street. I'm not that keen on shopping at the best of times, but among the jostling crowds in central London that day I was finding it more trying than usual.

While my family went to buy some Christmas decorations I escaped for a few minutes of peace and quiet. I wandered into a rather exclusive department store and took the escalator down to a different world. It was good to be away from the crowds.

The china department was beautifully laid out, with spotlighted dinner services, shelves full of delicate china, and figurines on pedestals. I looked at a few of the price tags: everything was out of my range.

I ambled past one of the enormous display cases and found, to my amazement, a potter stooping over his wheel. In his stained overalls he looked quite out of place in such a sumptuous setting! He was engrossed in his work.

A group of shop assistants meandered into the department; they were on their lunch break. For a while they stood and watched him, then one of the girls asked if she could have a try. He graciously stepped aside, and the girl moved over to the wheel and took the half-shaped clay.

She pressed the pedal, the wheel turned, and gradually the pot was formed. For some moments the crowd stood in amazement as the wet gray clay rose uncertainly above the wheel.

Suddenly the shape collapsed, fell off the wheel and

crumpled onto the floor beside her. Her clothes were splattered with clay and she looked annoyed. The group of shop girls laughed and sauntered away, their voices fading as they left the department.

I was just about to leave too, when I noticed the potter looking down at the lump of clay on the floor. He bent and patiently placed it back on the wheel. He set the wheel spinning, and in his eyes I could see the vision of what it would become.

His fingers moved deftly over the spinning mass; molding, guiding, forming. The clay slowly took shape. At last the wheel stopped. He had made a perfect vase. He gently removed it from the wheel and placed it on the workbench beside him. It was complete.

The Lord told the prophet Jeremiah to go and watch a potter at work. And as he watched, the potter took a misshapen piece of clay, and began to rework it. The potter took something ruined, and formed perfection from it. And the Lord said: "Haven't I the right to do with you people of Israel what the potter did with the clay?"

This Creator God who set the stars in place and who colored the rainbow's arch wants to shape our lives. This God, who made the world such a beautiful place, wants to make beautiful people too!

We can't make anything out of ourselves that has the right shape or purpose unless we place our lives in His hands. We may struggle and strain, we may exhaust ourselves in the heat of our effort, but we will only create disfigured lives.

This quality of submission is costly. Even Jesus found it to be so. There, in the Garden of Gethsemane, knowing that His death was near, He knelt and prayed, "Father, if You will, take this cup of suffering away from Me. Not My will, however, but Your will be done." In great anguish Jesus continued to pray until the sweat fell from His brow like great drops of blood.

When I was a student I lay on the floor of my college room in absolute brokenness. I recognized that I was utterly and completely dependent on Christ, and Him alone. I confessed that I was nothing and, in brokenness, cast myself upon His love.

Today, offer yourself like clay in the Potter's hand, and discover the shape your life should really be. For it is this quality of submission which should be at the center of your relationship with the Lord.

So don't you see that we don't owe this old do-it-yourself life one red cent. There's nothing in it for us, nothing at all. The best thing to do is give it a decent burial and get on with your new life. God's Spirit beckons. There are things to do and places to go!

This resurrection life you received from God is not a timid, grave-tending life. It's adventurously expectant, greeting God with a childlike "What's next, Papa?" God's Spirit touches our spirits and confirms who we really are. We know who he is, and we know who we are: Father and children.

Romans 8:12-16

O Searcher of hearts,
Thou knowest us better than we know ourselves,
and seest the sins which our sinfulness hides from
    us.
Yet even our own conscience beareth witness
    against us,
that we often slumber on our appointed watch;
that we walk not always lovingly with each
other,
and humbly with Thee;
and we withhold that entire sacrifice of ourselves
    to Thy perfect will,
without which we are not crucified with Christ,
or sharers in His redemption.
Oh, look upon our contrition,
and lift up our weakness,
and let the dayspring yet arise within our hearts,
and bring us healing, strength and joy.
Day by day may we grow in faith,
                    in self-denial,
                    in charity,
                    in heavenly mindedness.
And then, mingle us at last
with the heavenly host
of Thy redeemed for evermore.
Amen.

James Martineau (1805-1900)

SIX

when I've failed

On 29 November 1761 John Wesley wrote in his journal:

Many have, and many do daily experience an
unspeakable change. After being deeply convinced of
inbred sin, particularly of pride, anger, self-will and
unbelief, in a moment they feel all faith and love; no
pride, no self-will, or anger: and from that moment
they have continual fellowship with God, always
rejoicing, praying and giving thanks.

This work of transformation and change is an ongoing
process. On a number of occasions over the years I've had
to return to the Lord to ask Him to deal with aspects of
my being which I know have displeased Him. When I feel
that I've failed, I need to face up to my sin and remember

again the extent of His redeeming power.

The address read "The Chapel", and as there was no letter-box in the church, the postman had pushed it under the front doors as best he could. The contents of the letter were bewildering. The writer, using prison notepaper, begged me to go to a nearby prison to visit him.

A week later, after all the formalities had been completed, I was led down a long gray corridor and into a small interview cell. Keys rattled and the lock turned and I was led in to meet the prisoner. Two detectives arrived and sat behind me.

The prisoner had asked if he could make his confession to me, but with the police present. It was a horrific story of a murder and a life of sin. Eventually the man's life was transformed by the power of Christ. The prisoner could tell a new story: a story of repentance, forgiveness and of a new beginning.

I never cease to be amazed by the wonder of the Christian Gospel. No matter how low we have sunk, how far we have strayed, or how foolish a life we have lived, there is room in the love of Jesus for forgiveness and a new beginning. Many of us who are long-established Christians need to discover again the transforming power of this redemption.

I have a friend who is the minister of a small Yorkshire chapel. He is a keen artist, and often involves the whole congregation in celebrating their faith creatively.

One Sunday I watched as his congregation turned up with all kinds of rubbish they'd collected: scrap paper, empty boxes, and useless trash. Gradually they sorted through the refuse, and over the days that followed they discovered ways of using it artistically.

By the following Sunday the mound of rubbish had been transformed into a powerful illustration of the cross. The twisted, broken scraps of refuse had been redeemed into something beautiful and elegant.

This is the work of redemption. This is what the Lord wants to do within us all, if only we'll let Him. He wants to take away the filth and sin of our lives, and forgive us. He wants to take away the guilt and shame, and transform us. He wants to turn us away from selfishness, and redirect us.

The "Daybreak" musical tour was absolutely exhausting. Every day we traveled to a different town to set up several tons of equipment, rehearse the local choirs and drama groups, and present the musical to a packed theater.

In the production I played the part of Simon Peter. Night after night I had to stand alone on the stage in a blinding spotlight and enact "the denial."

As the last chords of the last song faded, the lengthy de-rig in Southampton Guildhall began. Props, costumes and PA equipment were packed and trundled on trolleys to the waiting truck.

I looked up at the Guildhall clock; it was just after midnight. It was my turn to travel overnight in the truck. I clambered into the cab next to the driver and wrapped my coat around me. We were bound for Cornwall . . . it was going to be a very long night.

The roads were covered with mist. The noise of the engine made conversation impossible; and no matter how I tried I couldn't find a comfortable position for sleep.

Hour after hour we rolled along in this kind of unreal world. My thoughts turned back to the previous evening's performance. The sounds and images rolled around my mind and I relived Peter's denial.

I looked again at my own life, and the words of Peter's denial returned to haunt me. The swirling mist in front of the headlights created an eerie feeling of unreality.

As my mind backtracked down the years I began to feel a failure as a disciple of Jesus. I felt that there were areas of my life which I still needed to yield to His Lordship. I felt that I loved the work more than I loved the Lord.

As soon as we arrived in Cornwall I found a room and knelt to pray. I was broken. I offered every aspect of my life and ministry back to the Lord and asked Him to change me from within.

Today, reflect on those aspects of your life which are not pleasing to the Lord. Do you really want to live in a continuing cycle of failure, selfishness and despair? Allow the Redeemer to transform those areas which you know are flawed; allow Him to change those wrong attitudes, that unyielded thought life, that root of selfishness and weakness. Hand over the trash in your life, and let Him get to work on redeeming you!

So if you're serious about living this new resurrection life with Christ, act like it. Pursue the things over which Christ presides. Don't shuffle along, eyes to the ground, absorbed with the things right in front of you. Look up, and be alert to what is going on around Christ—that's where the action is. See things from his perspective.

Your old life is dead. Your new life, which is your real life—even though invisible to spectators—is with Christ in God. He is your life.

Colossians 3:1-3

The nails were sharp
And the wood was rough
And the Cross was a cruel way to die

With no chance to repay,
To earn his way
Or to know the joy of forgiveness.

And the time dragged by,
With no hope of release,
From the pain or despair of the Cross.

With no chance to repay,
To earn his way
Or to know the joy of forgiveness.

And he gasped for breath
With a throat parched dry
"Remember me, Lord, when You're King."

With no chance to repay,
To earn his way
Or to know the joy of forgiveness.

How dare he believe,
That the King of kings
Might care for a thief like him?

With no chance to repay,
To earn his way
Or to know the joy of forgiveness.

And the King cried out
All over the world,
"Father—forgive them, I pray."

With no chance to repay,
Or to earn their way,
Let them know the joy of forgiveness!

And the King looked across
At the man born again
And the joy of a new creation.

With no chance to repay,
Or to earn his way
But knowing the joy of forgiveness.

SEVEN

when disappointments come

Once I visited the tiny island of Sark, which is a short boat ride from Guernsey. No cars are permitted on the island, but near the jetty where the ferry pulls in there is a taxi-rank of horses and carts.

Most of the "round the island tours" were beyond my price range, but at the very end of the line was an elderly driver with an elderly horse, and he offered to "do a deal"! The old man beamed at us with his one tooth, and explained that he'd only ever left Sark once—on a day trip to Guernsey. He hadn't enjoyed the experience!

The family and I climbed aboard the rickety old cart for a grand tour of the island. The horse clip-clopped ahead of us and the old cart rattled and shook as we drove along the dusty track.

As the tour progressed, the driver handed the reins over to my four-year-old son. I was worried. The boy hardly knew right from left, and as we drove past the cliff-tops I wondered if we might roll over! But when my son pulled right we turned right, and when he pulled left we turned left. The blinkered horse had no idea where he was headed; he simply obeyed. He trusted the driver implicitly. Jesus said, "Take My yoke and put it on you, and learn from Me, because I am gentle and humble in spirit; and you will find rest. For the yoke I will give you is easy, and the load I will put on you is light."

To be yoked to Christ means what it says. We are blinkered, and He steers. We don't know the road ahead, but He does. We are servants, but He is Master. As we actively seek His guidance for our lives, we discover what it means to be disciples.

We can't expect to plan our own lives in the Lord's service, nor choose the opportunities we think are best. We must actively seek the Lord's will and submit ourselves to it—even when we don't agree!

I ran out of Westminster Central Hall and hailed a passing taxi. I was devastated. The committee inside, after only a few moments of debate, had consigned eighteen months' work to the trash bin. By a vote of 13-9 a project to which I was passionately committed was rejected, and there was to be no right of appeal. We had faced commit-tee after committee and overcome hurdle after hurdle—but now it was all wasted and I was deeply disap-pointed.

I climbed into the taxi and sank back into the corner of the seat as we made the slow and frustrating journey to

Euston. I raced across the mezzanine and boarded the train to Preston with only minutes to spare.

As the train gathered speed I gazed out of the window in a kind of stupor. Soon the city sprawl was gone and the fields and trees flowed by. I mentally replayed the brief encounter in the committee room, wondering if I could have said something which might have changed the outcome. Tears filled my eyes. I couldn't believe that so much I'd hoped for would never be accomplished.

It was a horrendous journey. There were endless delays, a missed connection, and a growing unease that I might not reach Barrow in time for the evening service. It was nearly dark by the time I reached the city, and it took another frantic taxi ride to reach the church in time.

I walked in the door and followed the choir into the packed church for the start of the communion service. When at last I got up to preach I was still wrestling against the pain and turmoil of the day's events, and felt like not giving the sermon at all.

When the time came for me to make the appeal, I found that in some bizarre way I was talking to myself. The challenge of total surrender which I was laying before the congregation was actually something that I needed to hear for myself.

As I knelt at the communion table, with tears rolling down my cheeks, I realized again that what really mattered in my life was knowing the Lord. There and then I laid my work, my plans, and my ministry before Him. I looked up at the bread and wine and remembered again what love He had for me, and knew for sure that He was the mainspring of my ministry. We may not understand the disappointments and confusions of our lives, but when we wear the yoke of obedience we know that He will guide.

Today, submit to His will again. Offer your life to Him in full surrender and accept that, through all the confusions of the journey you travel, He knows the way ahead.

So let God work his will in you. Yell a loud no to the Devil and watch him scamper. Say a quiet yes to God and he'll be there in no time. Quit dabbling in sin. Purify your inner life. Quit playing the field. Hit bottom, and cry your eyes out. The fun and games are over. Get serious, really serious. Get down on your knees before the Master; it's the only way you'll get on your feet.

. . . And now I have a word for you who brashly announce, "Today—at the latest, tomorrow—we're off to such and such a city for the year. We're going to start a business and make a lot of money." You don't know the first thing about tomorrow. You're nothing but a wisp of fog, catching a brief bit of sun before disappearing. Instead, make it a habit to say, "If the Master wills it and we're still alive, we'll do this or that."

James 4:7-10, 13-15

Almighty God,
of Thy fullness grant to us
  who need so much,
  who lack so much,
  who have so little,
wisdom and strength.

Bring our wills unto Thine.
Lift our understandings
Into Thy heavenly light;

that we,
thereby beholding those things which are right,
and being drawn by Thy love,

may bring our will
and our understanding
together to Thy service,
until at last,
body and soul and spirit
may be all Thine,

and Thou be our Father,
and our Eternal Friend.
Amen.

         George Dawson (1821-1876)

EIGHT

when I don't want to meet the Lord

Sometimes, if I'm honest, I feel that there are high walls between me and the "holy place" of God's presence. I can open my Bible, go through the reading notes and scan my prayer list. But I haven't met the Lord. I can even go to church, sing the hymns, listen to the preacher, and sit through the service. But I haven't met the Lord.

Perhaps it's because I'm too busy, and my mind is racing around the schedule I'm facing. Or perhaps it's tiredness, and a preoccupation with my problems. At least, these are the excuses which I give myself.

In honest moments, however, I have to admit that the main reason is that I don't want to face the Lord. I know that I'm avoiding Him. When I reach a spiritual impasse like this I have to go on a long walk to sort things out with Him. I have my own favorite route, and on my personal pilgrimage I try to be honest with myself and with Him.

Recently, as I walked along a deserted country lane I struggled past my insecurity to claim His welcome . . . "Come to me, all of you." I knew that He hadn't closed the door on me. He was welcoming me into His presence with arms open wide. I stopped in a quiet clearing and entered into that holy place by faith in Him.

In my preoccupation with "instant quiet times" and "arrow prayers" I had lost the awesome sense of His holy presence. As I stood in the clearing I focused afresh on the holy majesty of my Lord and King. I recognized again that "otherness" of the Savior whom I serve. I quietly worshiped Him for who He is.

Gradually, an overwhelming sense of His power and presence washed over me as I stood peacefully before Him. Even as I lingered silently, I was aware that I was being changed by the experience.

I stood and praised Him and moved beyond the empty forms of words, beyond the familiar liturgies, beyond the tools of my evangelical spirituality to enter the holy place where Jesus is. The most wonderful place of all.

Teilhard de Chardin summed up the experience when he wrote: "Radiant Word, Blazing Power, you who mold the manifold so as to breathe your life into it, I pray you, lay on me your hands. Powerful and considerate, omnipresent, which plunge into the depths of the totality of my being through all that is most profound."

This is the place where broken hearts are healed. This is the place where the heavy load of sin is lifted. This is the place where the torture of worry is resolved. This is the place where marching orders are received and the way ahead discovered. This is the place where indescribable joy is found!

Some of us can go for days, months or even years without entering the holy place. We can maintain a regular prayer time, be frequent at worship, and remain consistent in Bible study. But we have not moved past the wall of our indifference to the holy place of His awesome presence.

Some years ago I visited the Wailing Wall in Jerusalem, a living reminder of the structure of the temple which had walls to keep out Gentiles, walls to keep out women, walls to keep out men and walls to keep out priests. Only the high priest could move beyond all the walls and enter the holy place . . . and then only once each year on the Day of Atonement.

Today, move beyond the walls of apathy which shut you out. The curtain is torn in two . . . the way is clear. You have access through Jesus Christ to enter the holy place— the most wonderful place of all.

"I'll forever wipe the slate clean of their sins."

Once sins are taken care of for good, there's no longer any need to offer sacrifices for them. So, friends, we can now— without hesitation—walk right up to God, into "the Holy Place." Jesus has cleared the way by the blood of his sacrifice, acting as our priest before God. The "curtain" into God's presence is his body.

So let's do it—full of belief, confident that we're presentable inside and out. Let's keep a firm grip on the promises that keep us going. He always keeps his word. Let's see how inventive we can be in encouraging love and helping

*out, not avoiding worshiping together as some do but spurring
each other on, especially as we see the big Day approaching.*
Hebrews 10:17-25

O God our Father,
who dost exhort us to pray,
and who dost grant what we ask,
if only, when we ask,
we live a better life;
hear me,
who am trembling in this darkness,

and stretch forth Thy hand unto me;
hold forth Thy light before me;
recall me from my wanderings;

and, Thou being my Guide,
may I be restored to myself and to Thee,
through Jesus Christ.
Amen.

St. Augustine (354-430)

NINE

when I'm not in a praising mood

A young minister from California came to stay at our church one summer. He brought with him a lively youth group called "The King's Kids" who were great fun to be with, and who had a joyous faith in Jesus.

Every morning I joined them for their devotional session in the local park. I'll never forget their commitment to praising the Lord, even when they were tired, or their mission wasn't going well. Praise was a part of who they were.

Time and again the writers of the Psalms urged their readers to make praise a way of life. The psalmist wrote: "I will bless the Lord at all times: his praise shall continually be in my mouth" (Ps. 34:1 KJV); and, "From the rising of the sun unto the going down of the same the Lord's name is to be praised" (Ps. 113:3 KJV).

The ancient community of Qumran, where the Dead Sea Scrolls were discovered, made it clear that praise is not something that rests on our changes of mood. Manual 10 of the Qumran rule of discipline says: "As long as I live it shall be a rule engraved on my tongue to bring praise like a fruit for an offering, and my lips as a sacrificial gift." The starting point for praise is a recognition of God's greatness and our unworthiness.

When the Israelites won a great victory over the Canaanite King Jabin, they praised the Lord! Deborah and Barak, the leaders of the people, worshiped together in awe of the great God who had given them victory. The word for praise used here was *barak*, which means "to kneel, to kneel down, or to salute."

When we enter the presence of the Lord, we should come in a *barak* attitude of reverence. When we praise Him, we remember our transience and mortality in the presence of His holiness, majesty, and immortality. We can only approach Him with humility.

One afternoon I attended sung evensong in Bath Abbey. As the April sunshine streamed in through the stained-glass windows, and the beautiful harmony of the choir filled the sanctuary, I sensed the presence of the Lord and knelt in adoration. I was kneeling because my heart was bowed before Him, and I was overwhelmed by a wonderful sense of His majesty and glory.

Sometimes, when we're not in that praising mood, we need to kneel before God and await His presence, and create space in our own lives for silence, meditation, reflection, and inner peace. We need moments when we can kneel before the Almighty and glimpse who He really is.

On a youth weekend in Derbyshire I stood with a group of about ninety people in a large field. It was nearly midnight, and the full moon was beaming from the clear night sky. It was so bright that it cast shadows around us. It had been a long day, I was tired, and I certainly wasn't in a praising mood!

But the sky was filled with millions of stars, and, as we stood together, a stillness descended upon us. We gazed in silent awe as the stars reached out into infinity and the enormity of the universe dwarfed us.

As we stood there in the open field we prayed out loud. God became very close, and we seemed to be standing on the edge of eternity. Our breath streamed out into the chill night air as we sang "Be still and know that I am God." In that moment I knew that I was in the presence of One much greater than I could ever imagine. I moved into a praising mood!

Praise is an attitude of heart and mind which needs to be cultivated. It demands energy, commitment, and effort—especially if we're tired or don't feel in a praising mood. Praise isn't something passive, but something actively given to God from the depths of our being.

Praise should not be quenched by the sadness of bereavement or the pain of suffering. Even when our earthly, human situation has changed for the worse, the living God has not. He is as worthy of praise today as He was before our troubles began!

As we discipline ourselves to praise Him and to glorify His name, we are lifted above our earthly situation and catch a glimpse of heaven. At times like these we see beyond the horizon of our human suffering and know the limitless resources of His love.

Today, discipline yourself to reach out in praise to the Lord. Catch a fresh glimpse of His majesty and power. Regain a right perspective on who He is . . . and who you are. His love and presence are the foundation of your life—a foundation which never moves.

We know that when these bodies of ours are taken down like tents and folded away, they will be replaced by resurrection bodies in heaven—God-made, not handmade—and we'll never have to relocate our "tents" again. Sometimes we can hardly wait to move—and so we cry out in frustration. Compared to what's coming, living conditions around here seem like a stopover in an unfurnished shack, and we're tired of it! We've been given a glimpse of the real thing, our true home, our resurrection bodies! The Spirit of God whets our appetite by giving us a taste of what's ahead. He puts a little of heaven in our hearts so that we'll never settle for less.

2 Corinthians 5:1-5

Hallelujah!
I ran through fields of green
I raced until the air rushed past my face
The clean air filled my lungs
I yelled for joy.
The cares of years had rolled away
I held my head up high
The weight upon my soul had gone
Free at last—
I knew that Jesus was alive—
Running with me
Living in my heart.
The Lord was with me in that moment of
    ecstatic living
The fear had gone
The frustrations of a lifetime blown away.
Free at last—
Nothing in this world or the next could ever
Bind me down again.
The Lord had set me free.
I filled my lungs and cried
Hallelujah . . . Jesus set me free!

. . . But that was yesterday.
I just don't feel that way right now.
I'm just not in that praising mood.
The sky is gray and dark again today
My work has got me down,
I'm tired . . .
And You seem far away.

But I remember yesterday,
And You are just the same.
Lord, You haven't changed.
You'll be the same forever.

And so I raise my head again,
And in the quiet of this evening hour,
I praise You, Lord.

T E N

when God seems far away

When I went forward as a candidate for the Methodist
ministry the committee which interviewed me asked me
to define "my experience of Christ." It was a difficult
question, and I didn't really know how to answer it. But I
talked of my relationship with the Lord and of the ways in
which I'd known Him in my life.

But there have been times in my life when I felt as if
the Lord had deserted me. Problems and demands have
crowded in, and my ability to cope with life has been
tested to the extreme. At times like this Watchman Nee's
simple explanation about the Christian life has really
helped me.

When he was describing his experience of Christ, he
took a very hot cup of tea, dropped a lump of sugar into it,

and stirred it well. "Now," he said to the young inquirer, "try and take the sugar out of the tea!"

His young friend was exasperated. "How can I? For the tea has become the sugar and the sugar has become the tea!"

"Exactly!" replied the great teacher. "In the same way, I am in Christ and He is in me."

This simple illustration has helped me to understand that even when everything is going wrong, I am immersed in Christ . . . and He in me. There is no aspect of my being which He doesn't know, and no detail of my situation of which He is unaware. If I could only see Him, Christ is incarnate in my situation with me.

The great Christian mystics of past centuries have talked about the experience of Christ as an essential part of Christian experience. Madam Guyon, writing at the end of the seventeenth century, wrote one of the greatest Christian classics on prayer. It's called *Experiencing the Depths of Jesus Christ.*

This book has enriched the lives of countless thousands of Christians down the centuries. She wrote:

> Dear child of God, all your concepts of what God is really like amount to nothing. Do not try to imagine what God is like. Instead, simply believe in His presence. Never try to imagine what God will do. There is no way God will ever fit into your concepts. What then shall you do? Seek to behold Jesus Christ by looking to Him in your inmost being, in your spirit.

It is this "believing in His presence" which has helped me through some of the hardest times of my Christian life.

I've had no evidence that He was with me—nothing tangible to go on, no bright flashing lights or thunderbolts—just an assurance that even in the worst times, He would be there.

My favorite account of the resurrection is the story of the walk to Emmaus. As the evening shadows lengthened, two disciples met a stranger who walked beside them. They were confused and sad, and invited the stranger to join them for supper.

They didn't know that the Lord was there, and had no evidence for His presence, but, as He broke the bread, the scales fell from their eyes and they saw. He had been alongside them all the time! Invisible . . . yet present.

It has been over twenty years since I first asked Jesus into my life, but my experience of Him has not dimmed in all that time. I have come to understand that wherever I go, the Lord is there. Whatever the future holds, He will give me the grace to face it.

I believe that He is with me in personal problems that seem insolvable. He is with me in family relationships when they are hard to handle. He is with me when life seems full of confusion. He can guide my path when I can see no way ahead. He is even with me when He seems far away.

All of us need to nurture this experience of Christ. It isn't enough to rush into His presence and gabble our lists of praise points and intercessory needs. We need to pause and share our hearts with Him. We need to give time to this relationship, and learn how to express our love for Him.

Today, turn to Christ again. He may seem far away,

but you are in Him, and He is in you. No matter how dark or confusing the times may be, He is with you still. Pause, and practice the presence of Christ.

Father, I want those you gave me
To be with me, right where I am,
So they can see my glory, the splendor you gave me,
Having loved me
Long before there ever was a world.
Righteous Father, the world has never known you,
But I have known you, and these disciples know
That you sent me on this mission.
I have made your very being known to them—
Who you are and what you do—
And continue to make it known,
So that your love for me
Might be in them
Exactly as I am in them.

John 17:24-26

The seasons come and go,
And I note their passing.
The cold gray of winter
Becomes the sunshine of spring.
The bare trees of December
Are filled by the lush green leaves of June.

The seasons of history come and go,
Empires fall away
And leaders process
Toward obscurity.
Fashions change,
Philosophies wither,
Causes fade away.

The seasons of my life
Come and go.
Yesterday I ran like a child
With the optimism of youth.
But time moves on.

The seasons come and go
But You are still here,
Lord of the seasons.
I rest again in the changeless season
Of Your eternal faithfulness.

ELEVEN

when I can't concentrate

My mind wanders mercilessly, often like a computer screen displaying the priorities for the week ahead: appointments to fulfill, phone calls to make, and mail to answer. It's often a real struggle for me to focus my mind, and I find I have to capture each wandering thought and bring it back into submission for the task of prayer!

I irritate myself with the vagaries of my own prayers. I can't "pray for Africa" or "pray for the poor" . . . there's nothing specific enough for me to focus my faith on here. I am constantly turning my own prayers into manageable and understandable requests, and that involves a mental process.

I can depress myself with long lists of the sad and the bad. I can create a cloud of despair by focusing too long on as yet unanswered requests. My prayers must be driven by hope, and as each petition forms in my mind it should have the drive of believing faith behind it.

Sometimes I am aware that my prayers are becoming opinions—paraded before the Almighty for His approval; diatribes which might win an argument, but are not pleasing to the Lord. Often I feel that I'm no good at prayer, and long for a greater fluency with the Lord. I need to harness my mind for the task of prayer.

The bus roared as it climbed up the steep hill beside the Sea of Galilee. Finally it reached the summit and turned into a lane beside the tree-lined church.

It was a quiet and beautiful place. My friends and I walked out onto the church veranda which overlooked the Sea of Galilee. We stood and gazed at the beauty of the rolling green hills reflected in the still blue waters of the lake. A thin mist in the distance gave an air of mystery to the scene. The stillness was almost tangible. Drifting from the church behind us came the muffled sound of singing. Time slowed to a stop, or so it seemed.

After some minutes we began to pray with eyes wide open. Jesus seemed so close, and the prayer natural and spontaneous. He was there, and we shared our thoughts with Him. This was true prayer: unassuming, personal, hushed, real; the kind of prayer He taught us to pray. Prayer from the mind, as well as the heart.

It was there on that hillside overlooking Galilee that Jesus said: "When you pray, do not use a lot of meaningless words, as the pagans do, who think that their gods will hear them because their prayers are long. Do not be like them. Your Father already knows what you need before you ask Him" (Matt. 6:7-8).

There is a simplicity about communicating with the Lord which should be sincere and uncomplicated. It is not the length of what we pray or the poetic phraseology which is important. True prayer comes from clear thoughts carefully formed in the mind.

Later, on the same trip, we entered a lovely white-walled garden on the Mount of Olives, where Jesus taught His disciples to pray:

Our Father which art in heaven,
Hallowed be thy name.
Thy kingdom come.
Thy will be done
in earth, as it is in heaven.
Give us this day our daily bread.
And forgive us our debts,
as we forgive our debtors.
And lead us not into temptation,
but deliver us from evil:
For thine is the kingdom,
and the power, and the glory,
for ever. Amen (Matt. 6:9-13 KJV).

We stood and watched pilgrims from around the world praying this prayer in a multitude of different languages. It was quite challenging to realize that these simple phrases bound us to the peoples of every tribe and tongue.

And then it was our turn. We gathered and recited the Lord's Prayer in English. It wasn't rushed, or repeated with cold familiarity. We spoke each phrase with reverence, and then we paused to ponder the meaning. Those oft-repeated words sounded new again as we breathed fresh faith into familiar phrases—each phrase so crisp, so clear, so profound. Jesus used the mind in prayer.

Prayer is not a gabble of hurried words and phrases. The pauses can be as significant as the words themselves. Prayer is not just idle chatter—it demands concentration. It is an act of the mind.

Saint Paul wrote: "What should I do, then? I will pray with my spirit, but I will pray also with my mind" (1 Cor. 14:15). Prayer doesn't just happen; it entails the engaging of mind as well as spirit!

Today, take control of your mind in prayer, for prayer demands work. Speak out what you feel. Articulate your needs. Direct your intercessions. Engage your intellectual powers. Say what's important. And He will hear.

So, when you pray in your private prayer language, don't hoard the experience for yourself. Pray for the insight and ability to bring others into that intimacy. If I pray in tongues, my spirit prays but my mind lies fallow, and all that intelligence is wasted. So what's the solution? The answer is simple enough. Do both. I should be spiritually free and expressive as I pray, but I should also be thoughtful and mindful as I pray. I should sing with my spirit, and sing with my mind.

1 Corinthians 14:13-15

God of Peace
Who brought again from the dead
our Lord Jesus Christ,
That great shepherd of the sheep,
By the blood of the eternal covenant:

Make us perfect
in every good work
To do Your will,

And work in us
that which is well pleasing
in Your sight;
Through Jesus Christ our Lord.

Hebrews 13:20-21

TWELVE

when I'm all "dried up"

I used to live near a park which was owned by the National Trust. It was quite wild and unkempt, like a piece of countryside in that London suburb. I loved to go there for prayer and meditation and walk beside a small stream. I loved the babble of the water on the pebbles in that tranquil place, and I often sensed the Lord's presence with me there.

As I was walking through the park one day I noticed that the Water Board had closed the floodgates, and that the stream was shut off. All that remained was a muddy channel. Flies hovered over it and it stank. I didn't stay long that day! It was all dried up.

It was a picture of how I felt in my life of prayer. I needed the renewing power of the Holy Spirit, the "stream of Living Water."

I'll never forget the day I visited a rather larger river—Niagara Falls! One of the most fascinating trips in the resort takes you behind the giant waterfall itself. The guide gave us raincoats, and then led us down dark passageways behind the falls. Eventually we reached a cavern and were able to look out through an opening to the daylight beyond.

The scene was indescribable. We were actually standing behind the huge torrent of water. The roar was deafening. Rainbows danced in the spray and we got soaked!

The guide explained that there were plans to build a hydroelectric turbine in the cave and to "turn off" the falls at night. The water would plunge through the turbine and create enough energy to light several whole states in North America. I found the concept mind-blowing. This one waterfall had the power to drive hundreds of factories and to light millions of homes!

But then I remembered the power of the Holy Spirit: the power that holds the stars in space; the power that holds the earth in orbit and brings the seasons in their turn. This is power without limit! The power of God! This is the healing stream which all of us need in our lives if we are to be effective Christians.

The Holy Spirit should be a never-ending stream welling up within each of us. Jesus said to the woman at the well, "The water that I will give him will become in him a spring which will provide him with life-giving water and give him eternal life" (John 4:14).

The prerequisites for the coming of the Holy Spirit upon us are basic indeed: repentance; forgiveness of our sins through the sacrificial death of Jesus; salvation; and a thirst for the Lord's renewing power, His personal gift to us and the seal of our relationship with Him.

I first heard about the renewal of the Holy Spirit when I was a student at Cliff College. I had been a committed Christian for some years, and all this talk about "renewal" was very new to me. Some of the noisy charismatic meetings which I attended really put me off, and I didn't think that it was for me.

Some months later we held a "quiet day" at the college—a day for silent meditation and reflection. I found it quite a strain because I am a natural talker. But during the afternoon I settled down to study the power of the Holy Spirit, and concluded that I needed this renewing power in my life.

That afternoon I wept before the Lord over my sin and pleaded with Him to fill me with the power of the Holy Spirit in a new way. As time went by I became aware that the Lord had filled me with new power, and I began to speak in strange tongues.

It was a new experience for me. Where my own earthly language ran out, I found a new way of expressing my love and devotion for the Lord. It was a matter of allowing the Spirit to help me to pray, and being released into a new freedom in worship, love and praise.

Today, as you meet the Lord in prayer, seek the renewing power of the Holy Spirit. Allow Him to fill you, to lift your prayers beyond the usual; to join with you in guiding you how to pray, and to empower you to praise the Lord in ways beyond your understanding. Receive the never-ending stream into your life.

I will talk to the Father, and he'll provide you another Friend so that you will always have someone with you. This Friend is the Spirit of Truth. The godless world can't take him in because it doesn't have eyes to see him, doesn't know what to look for. But you know him already because he has been staying with you, and will even be in you!

John 14:16-17

O God, the King of glory,
who hast exalted Thine only Son Jesus Christ
with great triumph
unto Thy kingdom in heaven;

We beseech Thee, leave us not comfortless;
but send to us Thine Holy Ghost to comfort us,

and exalt us into the same place
whither our Savior Christ is gone before,

who liveth and reigneth with Thee and the
Holy Ghost,
one God, world without end.
Amen.

The Collect for the Sunday after Ascension Day
The Book of Common Prayer

THIRTEEN

when I doubt my faith

There are times when I question my faith, and wonder how it really works. When doubt threatens my relationship with the Lord I turn back and remember the early days of my relationship with Him.

When I was a few months old my mother used to take me on her preaching engagements! Apparently, when I cried, she would rock my carry-cot with her foot in the pulpit, in the hope that I would go to sleep!

I am deeply grateful for the Christian home in which I was reared; for the daily prayers at my bedside, and for the encouragement to serve the Lord which my parents constantly gave.

But I was bored and fed up with church life by the time I was a teenager. I preferred to ride my bike around the park than be in Sunday School. I had been taken to church since my earliest childhood days, and I'd had enough of it all.

My cherished memories of Sunday School were of the pranks I played rather than the lessons I learned. I remember being asked to stand in the corridor in my primary class for mucking up the Lord's Prayer; and I got into trouble in the senior group for tying a girl's long ponytail to the chair-back!

I knew everything about Christianity by my midteens, but I hadn't met the Savior. I had been to so many church meetings that I knew the Bible well, but I didn't really know Jesus at all.

One weekend our youth group went to a camp in the village of Alvechurch, just outside Birmingham. It was there that I began to see beyond my Sunday School religion. In the quietness of the woods I prayed, "I'm not sure if I can accept it all or believe it all, Lord . . . but if You are real, show me."

I moved from a vague kind of belief in God to a living faith in Christ very slowly during the following year. It was a period of much discussion, study and prayer.

First, I had to accept intellectually that Jesus existed as a real person. I read up on history and began to discover that there was evidence for Christ's life and ministry in the writings of early Jewish historians such as Josephus.

At the teenage discussion group I went to, I started out as the argumentative skeptic in the group, but I gradually became more and more convinced that Jesus was someone very special.

I remember the words of Peter making a particular impression on me. "We have not depended on made-up stories in making known to you the mighty coming of our

Lord Jesus Christ. With our own eyes we saw His greatness. We were there when He was given honor and glory by God the Father" (2 Peter 1:16-17).

I began to realize that Jesus was far more than just a "nice guy." The more I asked questions about Him and heard about Him, the more I wanted to know Him in a real way myself.

I came to see that no one throughout history could be compared to Him; the effect of His life on individuals and on nations is immeasurable. Here was someone who not only preached forgiveness, but who hung on a cross to prove it!

My Christian friends convinced me to take Jesus seriously, and to search for Him with all my heart. As I met more and more believers, I began to want the kind of relationship with Jesus which they so obviously had.

I knew that my intellectual assent to Jesus was not enough because I hadn't really put my faith in Him. Things came to a head when we went back to the youth camp at Alvechurch at Easter. On Easter Sunday morning I heard a very elderly deaconess preach about the risen Jesus, and the story of the Resurrection suddenly made sense to me.

After lunch I took time out from the rest of the group and went for a walk in the woods. I found the same place in the wood where I had prayed before, but this time I prayed, "Lord, I give You my life. All that I am, and all I ever hope to be." I knelt and asked Jesus Christ to be my Friend and Savior.

For the first time I glimpsed the reality of the living Savior who died for me and who could enter my life in a new and powerful way. There was no dramatic experience, just a new sense of peace and closeness to Jesus. Before my conversion, Jesus seemed far away, high up—as if on the mountaintop. He was distant and unknowable, and He couldn't even be reached in prayer.

But when I came to know Jesus for myself He came down from the mountaintop and began to walk the valley by my side. He became my personal Friend—always there to share whatever joys or sorrows may come my way.

There, in the stillness of the forest, I met Jesus Christ. He became a real Friend to me and for the first time I believed His great promise: "I will never leave you nor forsake you." I took Him at His word.

Soon afterward, I stuck a sign on my bedroom door which read, "Tell Jesus." Whenever I went out of the door I couldn't help but see it. Sometimes I went out of the door to take an exam, and was enduring that awful nerve-racking feeling that precedes exams! As I went out of the door the sign reminded me to "Tell Jesus." At other times I went out of the door feeling great as I went to meet my girlfriend. The sign reminded me that in every situation Jesus was there to share my life with me. Knowing Jesus is what real Christianity is all about!

My relationship with Jesus is at the center of my life. There have been many times when I've failed Him and let Him down, but He has never let go of me, and He's always brought me back.

Today, go back over the years of your discipleship and remember those early days of your faith. Move back beyond the complexity of theology or the confusions of church life. Move back before the troubles of your present situation. Taste again the simple sweetness of His presence.

But if God himself has taken up residence in your life, you
can hardly be thinking more of yourself than of him. Anyone,
of course, who has not welcomed this invisible but clearly
present God, the Spirit of Christ, won't know what we're talking about. But for you who welcome him, in whom he
dwells—even though you still experience all the limitations of
sin—you yourself experience life on God's terms. It stands to
reason, doesn't it, that if the alive-and-present God who raised
Jesus from the dead moves into your life, he'll do the same
thing in you that he did in Jesus, bringing you alive to himself?
When God lives and breathes in you (and he does, as surely as
he did in Jesus), you are delivered from that dead life. With his
Spirit living in you, your body will be as alive as Christ's!

Romans 8:9-11

So, what is this life about?
A lifestyle timetable,
Planned precisely week by week,
With variations on bank holidays?

What is this life about?
Following forefathers
Down well-worn paths of habit . . .
Without asking where they lead?

What is this life about?
Doing . . . instead of being?
Living for kicks . . .
instead of living for life itself?

Existing in lonely monochrome.
Missing the Technicolor friendship God
    intended?

FOURTEEN

when I need forgiveness

If only we could see ourselves as Christ sees us: the walls of prejudice that have built up; the bad habits that we cling to; the hurt that is festering within us; the evil motives we've whitewashed with good intentions; the deep-rooted self-centeredness.

I am convinced that where there are unresolved issues such as these in our personal lives, we are unable to enjoy a full relationship with Jesus. Jesus said, "So if you are about to offer your gift to God at the altar and there you remember that your brother has something against you, leave your gift there in front of the altar, go at once and make peace with your brother, and then come back and offer your gift to God" (Matt. 5:23-24).

There are so many things which the Lord needs to

change within us if we are to approach His holy presence. Some Christians seem to think that we need offer our lives to Him only once, but I find that I need to come back to be forgiven and cleansed again and again.

When I was a student at Cliff College I used to do manual work on the college grounds a couple of times a week. The hours I spent in the garden were a good break from study, though I am no gardener! We used to talk and discuss as we worked—after all, a solid afternoon of weeding can be rather backbreaking!

One day I was working with a student who I felt was close to the Lord. We talked about our relationship with Christ, and I asked him about his faith. He told me that every week he spent an hour alone in the college chapel. He called it his weekly "sorting-out session" with the Lord. During that hour he would lay his life open before God and ask the Holy Spirit to pinpoint areas where he had failed. He told me that he would then confess his sins, claim forgiveness and ask the Lord to change him.

I've never forgotten that conversation, and ever since, I've seen confession as far more important than a "sorry" prayer said before communion. The Lord's refining, purifying, recreating process should be continuing in all of our lives each week, and this demands time given over to honesty with God.

Each time I stop for a "sorting-out session" with the Lord, I find new areas of my life which need to be yielded to Him. I need to learn how to rely more on Him and less on myself. I need to receive the helpful and positive criticism of others. I want the lessons I learn from failure to become a growth point in my Christian life. I really do want Him to correct the wrong attitudes which so affect me.

If we are to face up to the reality of our sin we need to be really specific. It was the custom for people at Wesley's class meetings to confess their sins to each other and to encourage one another in the life of holiness. This was real confession—heartfelt, embarrassing, humbling. The Lord can really work with people who are willing to be honest with Him.

We need to be specific in our prayers of confession. Sometimes I've even made a written list of sins and asked the Lord to deal with them one by one. It can be a painful experience, but one which is a vital aspect of the life of prayer.

When Jesus cried, "It is finished!" He said it all. He wasn't saying, "I'm finished," but rather, "I've finished the work that I came to do." The sacrifice was complete, and by dying on the cross He had won salvation for us. We receive this forgiveness as a free gift or we don't receive it at all. We can certainly never deserve it.

When I have a "sorting-out session" with the Lord, I aim for it to be honest, real and thorough. Unless I lay my life before the Lord and allow the searchlight of His holiness to rest upon me, these wrong things in my life can never be dealt with.

Today, lay your life before the Lord and ask Him to reveal those things which need to be changed. Be real with Him, be honest with Him—and come with a willingness to change. Ask Him to begin a purifying and cleansing work within you. Allow Him to make you more like Jesus.

So, chosen by God for this new life of love, dress in the wardrobe God picked out for you: compassion, kindness, humility, quiet strength, discipline. Be even-tempered, content with second place, quick to forgive an offense. Forgive as quickly and completely as the Master forgave you. And regardless of what else you put on, wear love. It's your basic, all-purpose garment. Never be without it.

Let the peace of Christ keep you in tune with each other, in step with each other.

Colossians 3:12-15

How we break the World!
The first commandment is:
"Love the Lord your God with all your heart,
*   soul, mind and strength."*
But we don't . . .
We ignore our Creator.
We break the world.
We love our possessions.
We explain all things without God.
We are strong enough to destroy the planet!
We have broken our promises,
We have broken the world,
We are breaking our Father's heart,
And yet He loves us.

For God so loved the world that He gave His only
*   Son, Jesus Christ.*
The Lord our God can give new life.
He restores my soul.
We see His healing hands at work in all creation.
We hear His call to turn to Him
And start again.

The second commandment is:
"Love your neighbor as yourself,"
But we don't . . .
We allow our differences
To spring up between us.
We build high walls of suspicion . . .
And hide behind our barriers of hostility . . .
We would rather cross the street
Than meet each other face to face.

We have broken our promise to love our
    neighbors,
We have broken the world,
We are breaking our Father's heart,
And yet He goes on loving us . . .

He calls us to break down the barriers
To demolish the walls that separate us;
To reach out our hands to each other
And to restore our unity . . .
He calls us to turn from bitterness
And start again . . .

He calls us to mend the world . . .
The world He made . . .
The world He dies to save . . .

FIFTEEN

when I can't hear God

The technical word for listening to God is "meditation", and I've had some disastrous experiences of it! Some of my attempts at meditation have been an opportunity for my mind to focus on anything but the presence of the Lord.

Once I was asked to meditate on a candle, and was given no direction for my mind to follow. I ended up thinking about candles rather than the Lord! For me, the most effective kind of meditation is when I fix my mind on the Word of God; when I concentrate on some passage of Scripture which is rich in meaning and which has a direct bearing on my Christian life.

If I look at a candle as I meditate on the words, "Jesus said, 'I am the Light of the world'," those words begin to come to life for me in a completely new way. My mind is focused on the word, not the symbol. True meditation leads us beyond what we are looking at and into the presence of the Lord. These things are a means to prayer and not an end in themselves.

For me, one of the greatest joys of meditation is when some aspect of the Gospel lights up in a way that's just for me. So there is no agenda in meditation, just an openness to hear the Word and to apply it to my own specific situation. If I don't give time and space to listening, I might just miss what God's trying to tell me.

When the Lord spoke to Jonah, he wasn't listening. The Lord asked him to go and preach to the people of Nineveh, but he didn't hear. Anyway, it was a pagan city and he knew he wouldn't be welcome there.

Jonah compromised his call. He was willing to uproot and travel overseas as a missionary, but he wanted to choose the location. Tarshish was more convenient . . . more his kind of place. He wasn't listening.

By stepping out of the Lord's will he ended up in the wrong place at the wrong time. But at last, when Jonah was in the pit of the whale's belly, the Lord had his undivided attention!

The time was ripe for the people of Nineveh to respond to God's message, and if he hadn't gone there he would never have known. Because Jonah wasn't listening, he nearly missed God's plan for his life.

Prayer is not only about talking, it's about listening— creating space for inner quietness so that God's voice can be heard amid all the other voices that call for our attention.

Several times each week I go on a prayerwalk. I attempt to leave behind the cares and pressures of the day and to make a journey of discovery with the Lord. I leave the chatter of the world, turn off my car radio, and trudge out along country lanes in order to hear God's voice.

I find it important to distance myself from the thoughts that fill my mind, and to focus on things more important than the appointments of the day. It's my attempt to rise above the dross of what seems urgent—to glimpse the things that are really significant. There can be a world of difference between the two! As I breathe fresh air and walk on new paths I try to open my mind to hear the voice of the Lord.

I must admit I do have an overactive mind. I need this space to focus on the Word of God and to concentrate on Him, or else I never get beyond the pressures of the day to hear what God is saying. When I walk like this the Lord sometimes speaks to me through inner conviction. I can't describe it, except that it's stronger than a "hunch", and this feeling may return again and again until eventually I respond to it.

Sometimes this conviction is telling me that something is right, and there is some course of action that I need to follow. The conviction only disappears when I finally say "yes." But it can also come as a warning that something is wrong, and I remain uneasy until I say "no." I am in no doubt that the Lord uses this sensitivity to His guidance in many ways.

Once I was invited to become the minister of a church in the north of England and I went to visit it. When I returned home I had a niggling sense of unease about the invitation. Everything about the situation seemed so right, but I didn't feel easy.

I went to see some mature Christian friends who were willing to spend time with me, thinking and praying about

God's will for my life. I shared my nagging doubts with them and as we prayed together they confirmed my response. I didn't go.

Listening to the Lord is a really important activity, and before we make plans or decide on major changes in our lives we should devote quality time to it. Listening to God should always be accompanied by reading His Word and by sharing with other believers—important checks that what we're hearing is what He is really saying.

Today, don't burst into God's presence, say too much and listen too little. Take the opportunity to hear what the Lord wants to say through His Word. Quiet your heart and mind, and concentrate on the Lord. Let Him do the talking.

Don't fret or worry. Instead of worrying, pray. Let petitions and praises shape your worries into prayers, letting God know your concerns. Before you know it, a sense of God's wholeness, everything coming together for good, will come and settle you down. It's wonderful what happens when Christ displaces worry at the center of your life.

Summing it all up, friends, I'd say you'll do best by filling your minds and meditating on things true, noble, reputable, authentic, compelling, gracious—the best, not the worst; the beautiful, not the ugly; things to praise, not things to curse. Put into practice what you learned from me, what you heard and saw and realized. Do that, and God, who makes everything work together, will work you into his most excellent harmonies.
Philippians 4:6-9

Practical advice

1. Find a quiet place, and as you walk or stop to look at things let your whole being relax.
2. Allow the meaning of the Scripture to penetrate your heart and mind, constantly praying, "Lord, speak to me."
3. A few minutes are probably enough at first—the time can be extended with experience.

Some possible forms for meditation

1. The night sky filled with stars:
   "You must shine among them like stars lighting up the sky, as You offer them the message of life" (Phil. 2:15-16).
2. A stream babbling over pebbles—or a glass jug full of water:
   "The water that I will give him will become in him a spring which will provide him with life-giving water and give him eternal life" (John 4:14).
3. A loaf of bread:
   "I am the bread of life . . . He who comes to Me will never be hungry; he who believes in Me will never be thirsty" (John 6:35).
4. A sunrise:
   "The Lord's unfailing love and mercy still continue, fresh as the morning, as sure as the sunrise. The Lord is all I have, and so I put my hope in Him" (Lam. 3:22-24).
5. Mountains and skies:
   "Can anyone measure the ocean by handfuls or measure the sky with his hands? Can anyone hold

the soil of the earth in a cup or weigh the mountains and hills on scales? Can anyone tell the Lord
what to do?" (Isa. 40:12-13).

SIXTEEN

when I'm disillusioned

When we start out as Christians many of us are aware that Jesus is the focus of it all. We have the kind of faith that can move mountains. Our prayers are alive and specific, and we look with eagerness to see how the Lord will answer them. Our faith matches the classic definition found in Hebrews 11:1: "To have faith is to be sure of the things we hope for, to be certain of the things we cannot see."

After a while, however, life can drag us down and our simplicity of faith may disappear. Disillusionment can wrap itself around our thinking, praying, and planning, and we can become cold and half-hearted in the life of prayer.

I have seen this kind of disillusionment in so many who are heavily involved in church life. Youth leaders who have slogged on year after year, and who have grown tired and fed up. Enthusiasm has dwindled and faith has become dull.

Some ministers have spent years coping with entrenched attitudes and petty traditionalism, and it is easy for disillusionment to take root in situations like this. Service for the Lord can make us fed up with everything and everyone. The ministry can become a burden. There have been times in my own life when I've felt exhausted and too fed up to pray.

Once I was visited by an older and wiser minister. He told me that I was trying to do too much, too soon. He showed me that I'd been setting targets for myself which were not the Lord's, and that I'd been racing toward goals that He was not asking me to reach!

Whatever sphere of Christian service we may be involved in, we can shoulder burdens which we have not been asked to bear. It's easy for our Christianity to become all works and no faith! We can lose our grip on Jesus.

Once, when I was on a hike with my two sons, we took a wrong turn. I don't know how it happened because the nature trail we'd been following was clearly marked and the pathway should have been easy to follow! We must have been distracted and turned right instead of left—my navigation skills are not very good at the best of times! Before long we were completely lost and wondered if we should press on or turn back. My sons looked at me in desperation—they'd been in this situation with me before!

We pressed on, but the path got narrower and narrower until I had to carry my youngest son through a bed of stinging nettles. It was obvious that we had left the beaten track and turned off into the wilderness.

When work for the Lord becomes more important

than the Lord Himself, and when our commitment is to the "ministry" rather than to Him, we've left the path and strayed into the wilderness. We need to reassess our work for the Lord and ask whether it has become too dominant. We must retrace our steps to discover why we do the work at all.

I stood in quiet reverence. I had reached the destination of my journey. The long hours of travel and the many weeks of preparation were behind me. I was standing beside the Garden Tomb in Jerusalem.

This spot had become the focal point for my travels; the place where I would pause to remember the events of that first Easter morning. "Come," said the elderly guide, "step inside and see—the tomb is empty."

I stepped into the cave and turned to look out to the beautiful garden beyond. In my mind I reran the events of Easter morning. I saw Mary Magdalene approaching the tomb with the spices in her hand. I saw her surprise at finding the body gone. I heard her cry of despair to the gardener: "They have taken my Lord away, and I do not know where they have put him!"

But this was no gardener. This was the risen Lord. Christ had overcome the power of death and opened the way to eternal life. Christ had risen triumphant over the power of evil, and anticipated the final victory. Christ had defeated the power of suffering, and risen victorious to be our source of renewing strength. Jesus Christ had risen from the dead! I knew again that He was the source of my faith, my ministry and my life.

Today, instead of focusing on all the responsibilities that press hard upon you, focus on Jesus. Spend time with

Him and you will discover what He wants of you and you will receive the strength to do it. Let Him grow bigger and your work grow smaller and you will rediscover the reason why you serve Him.

Then he told them what they could expect for themselves: "Anyone who intends to come with me has to let me lead. You're not in the driver's seat—I am. Don't run from suffering; embrace it. Follow me and I'll show you how. Self-help is no help at all. Self-sacrifice is the way, my way, to finding yourself, your true self. What good would it do to get everything you want and lose you, the real you? If any of you is embarrassed with me and the way I'm leading you, know that the Son of Man will be far more embarrassed with you when he arrives in all his splendor in company with the Father and the holy angels."

Luke 9:23-26

Mary's Speech

Listen! Listen to me!
I do love Jesus, He is important to me.
Before I met Him, my life was a mess—I was
    demon possessed.
I know that now.

I thought I had everything—money, lovers,
    excitement . . .
But knowing Jesus made it all seem sordid and
    empty.
But Jesus cast out my demons.

It was like being a swept room—clean, and
    ordered.
And now I have turned to Him—He has filled
    up my life.
He's given me self-respect.

If Jesus could care for me--
Not for my money or my body . . .
I must be important.
He cared for me. He really cared!

Then I saw Him on the cross.
My life's purpose seemed to drip out
with the blood falling from His hands and feet.
And when He cried, "My God, My God why
    have You forsaken Me?"
I cried the same at God.
How could this happen?

He was so good.
I loved Him . . . and watched Him die.
I saw them put the spear in His side.
I came to the tomb this morning
expecting to find a dead man.
What else could I think?
I didn't even believe when the stone was rolled away
and the angel spoke . . .

Then He spoke . . .
"Mary," He said.
I was overwhelmed.
I wanted to hold Him.
I don't pretend to understand it all
But I am not mad.
He was there—in the garden.
I saw Him.
I heard Him.
It is Him who makes my life worth living.
And He told me to tell you that He is alive.
He is alive!

SEVENTEEN

when I think God's forgotten me

Jacob was running away from home, and leaving behind him all that was most precious and important to him. He felt alone, confused and afraid, for he was facing an unknown future. Far from anywhere, out in the wilderness, he used a stone for his pillow and fell asleep.

As he slept he saw a vision of the angels of heaven ascending and descending a ladder which stretched from earth to the very throne of God. In this dream the Lord assured him, "Remember, I will be with you and protect you wherever you go, and I will bring you back to this land."

Jacob suddenly realized that the Lord was with him in the personal problems which seemed so insolvable; with him in the family conflicts and the broken relationships; with him in the confusing decisions which he didn't know how to make.

Jacob had sensed the presence of the Lord in a place that he didn't expect and in a way that had taken him by surprise. After he awoke he took the stone that had been his pillow, poured olive oil over it to set it apart as holy, and called the place "Bethel", which means "House of God." The stone was a symbol that God was with him— even when he felt forgotten.

Too many of us have come to think of prayer as something separate from life itself, and that we can only pray when we kneel piously in some "holy place." But prayer is far wider than this, for the Bible teaches that the whole of life is a celebration of God's presence with us. There is no segregation between sacred and secular. Any place can be our "Bethel."

Prayer is about shopping in the supermarket and driving on congested roads. It's about family relationships and caring for awkward colleagues. It's the frustration of difficult work, and the joy of a job well done. It's celebrating the presence of God in the nitty-gritty of everyday routine. Prayer is life itself!

"Everything you do or say," wrote Paul, "should be done in the name of the Lord Jesus, as you give thanks through Him to God the Father" (Col. 3:17). A life which reflects the presence of the Lord is a life of prayer. It's a personality stamped with the Transcendent. It's living a daily relationship with Jesus Christ, the Son of God. It's knowing that wherever you go and whatever you do, He remembers you.

I entered the ancient monastery and ambled down the long shady veranda and found the tomb of the early church leader St. Ignatius. I gazed in wonder at the beau-

tiful scrolls near his tomb, some of which dated back
fifteen hundred years.

As I strolled around this ancient place I sensed the
eternal nature of my Heavenly Father. I saw my life in the
perspective of God's vast purposes and my work as but a
fragment of His immense design. As I meandered around
the shady courtyard I was overwhelmed by a sense of
God's infinite greatness and my own tiny insignificance.

But then I looked down and saw the figure of a tiny
dead sparrow, and Christ's words confronted me: "Aren't
five sparrows sold for two pennies? Yet not one sparrow is
forgotten by God . . . so do not be afraid; you are worth
much more than many sparrows."

That tiny lifeless body conveyed God's love for me. In
an instant I glimpsed the vastness of my Heavenly Father's
love, and I saw that His care for all that He has made
spans undimmed across the centuries. For this is the God
who cares about sparrows, and this is the God who cares
about me. I am not forgotten.

I recognized that there is no part of me outside
His knowledge and concern; no aspect of my life He
doesn't understand and no insecurity of which He's
unaware. As I looked at the sparrow I recognized that my
every breath is a gift of God and that my being is mysteriously bound up with His. He remembers me.

The early church father Gregory wrote: "All that
abides, abides in you alone, the movement of the universe
surges toward you—of all beings you are the goal. No
matter where you may be, as long as your soul forms the
sort of resting place in which God can dwell and linger,
He will visit you."

Today, let the whole of your life be a prayer. Let every

place you visit become your "Bethel." Let everything you think and everything you say be pleasing to the Lord. Let there be no distance between the sacred and the secular. Celebrate God with you in the here and now. Find Him in unlikely places. Seek Him in the midst of hectic activity, and find Him present in stressful situations. For this is our God: before us, behind us, above us, beside us and, best of all, within us still. This is our God—who never leaves us nor forsakes us—and who never ever forgets us.

Jesus said . . . "It's who you are and the way you live that count before God. Your worship must engage your spirit in the pursuit of truth. That's the kind of people the Father is out looking for: those who are simply and honestly themselves before him in their worship. God is sheer being itself—Spirit. Those who worship him must do it out of their very being, their spirits, their true selves, in adoration."

The woman said, "I don't know about that. I do know that the Messiah is coming. When he arrives, we'll get the whole story."

"I am he," said Jesus. "You don't have to wait any longer or look any further."

John 4:23-26

From distant civilizations long gone to dust
You watch me now.
From future generations yet unborn
You come to me.
You stride across the centuries
And watch my earthly pilgrimage.
You see my life
From birth, to death
And in an instant see me come and go.

And so I look out
from this fleeting moment
and glimpse eternity.
And know again
That you,
My God,
Remember me.

EIGHTEEN

when I can't pray in church

All kinds of things irritate me about the way in which prayers are led in church, and I really have to discipline myself not to tune out. Some preachers gabble their prayers at such a rate that I just can't keep pace—I'm only on the first petition when they are on number five. I don't try to keep up. I just tune in to odd words and phrases and try to make them my own.

Other preachers launch into prayer without a pause. They close their eyes and open their mouths to fill the silence. I find it is essential to spend a short time "practicing the presence of God" before I can pray. I must prepare myself, and if it means that I miss the opening phrases of the preacher's prayer, I don't really worry.

The unspecific prayers irritate me too! We pray "for

Africa" or "for the poor", but I find it impossible to exert
faith for prayers as vague as these. I find myself turning
such prayers into more manageable and specific requests,
especially picturing people who I know are involved in
the situation mentioned.

Then there are depressing prayers: long lists of the sad
and the bad; prayers that leave a cloud of despair over the
worship; prayers without hope. There is no explosion of
believing faith within us and everyone feels depressed.

And there are prayers which aren't prayers at all:
camouflaged sermons; opinions paraded before the
Almighty for approval; diatribes to which we're supposed
to say "Amen." I find these prayers the hardest of all, and
sometimes I feel obliged to turn away and pray alone.

I frankly admit, therefore, that I find the prayers in
corporate worship really hard. The words "Let us pray"
sometimes make me want to tune out. Prayer in church is
often cold and mechanical.

I guess it's easy to criticize preachers for being self-
indulgent when they pray, but the use of empty phrases
without thought or preparation is irritating in the
extreme. And even powerful prayers from books can be
read in a cold and formal way without life and faith.

But perhaps the greatest fault lies in us, the members
of the congregation. It's so easy for us to come to prayer in
worship with no desire to meet the living God. Corporate
prayer demands a deep commitment of mind in concentration and of heart in faith. Prayer in worship demands
effort on the part of every worshiper, and too many of us
are just sitting back and expecting prayer to "happen"
without our input of faith.

It isn't easy to love the Lord "with all your mind"

(Luke 10:27), particularly if your mind has a will of its own! Sometimes in church my mind becomes a visual display unit charting priorities for the week ahead. Appointments to fulfill, phone calls to make and mail to answer! In focusing my mind during corporate prayer I have to try to turn each wandering thought into a prayer, and then return again to listen to the lead prayer as quickly as I can!

I try to identify with the one who is leading us in prayer and to make their expressions my own. And I do my utmost to encourage them, even if it's only with a hearty "Amen!" I try to remember that corporate prayer, even when it's at its most frustrating, is communication with the Lord and has the potential to change all things.

Praying in church should lift us beyond the whisper of children's voices, rustling candy wrappers, coughs and sneezes, and enable us to meet the living Savior. We should know the reality of His presence and the joy of real communion with Him.

When the disciples couldn't drive out a demon from the young boy, they couldn't understand what had gone wrong. "It was because you haven't enough faith," answered Jesus. "I assure you that if you have faith as big as a mustard seed, you can say to this hill, 'Go . . .'" (Matt. 17:20). Prayer doesn't need much faith—only a mustard seed's worth will do! But forms of words without the force of faith are meaningless indeed.

As we participate in congregational prayer we should aim to fill the prayers with faith. As a congregation we add our "mustard seeds" of faith together, and prayers in church become the opportunity for a corporate release of faith. Prayer in church should be the time to move mountains and to see God's hand at work. Praying in church is hard work—but it's the body communicating with the Head. A time to meet the Lord and a time to change the world.

Next time you're in church, listen to the prayers, live the words, and add the energy of your faith to that of the one who prays them!

So, friends, we can now—without hesitation—walk right up to God, into "the Holy Place." Jesus has cleared the way by the blood of his sacrifice, acting as our priest before God. The "curtain" into God's presence is his body.

So let's do it—full of belief, confident that we're presentable inside and out. Let's keep a firm grip on the promises that keep us going. He always keeps his word. Let's see how inventive we can be in encouraging love and helping out, not avoiding worshiping together as some do but spurring each other on, especially as we see the big Day approaching.

Hebrews 10:19-25

Grand cathedrals,
Tin huts.
Chants and choirs and quietness,
Choruses and commotion.
The people are at prayer.

Order
Unpredictability
High church
Low church
And churches in between.

Then, suddenly,
Unexpectedly.
The Guest arrives.

He organizes that,
Not us.
Thank God.

And where the two or three
Are praying in His Name,
He comes.

NINETEEN

when I'm not listening

Many of us consider ourselves "off duty" in the Christian life when we're not actively involved in Christian work or devotion. Unfortunately, this means that we're making large areas of our lives "out of bounds" to the Lord.

This attitude can mean that we're not listening to the Lord for whole sections of the week. Consequently, we're missing out on some of the most rewarding opportunities that He has in store for us!

Philip the evangelist was someone who listened for the Lord. He had just finished a mission in the capital city of Samaria. It had been an effective time during which many had heard the Gospel. Mission work like this leaves you elated but drained, and I imagine that he was completely exhausted.

It was then, at the end of the mission, that Philip

received God's word to go and stand beside the desert road linking Jerusalem and Gaza. It must have seemed a crazy command, but Philip heard the call and was ready to obey. The rest of the story is well known: an Ethiopian official passed that way and Philip led him to Christ. And all because he had heard the Lord's command.

I'll never forget what happened one dark, snowy afternoon in Yorkshire. I was out on my rounds in the mining village where I was minister. I had spent three hours visiting the "shut-ins", and it was nearly time to go home. I was on my last visit of the afternoon and I bade farewell to the frail old lady and trudged through the snow to my car. I had finished my visiting list and was ready for a break. The roads were treacherous and the wheels of the car slithered as I drove through the snow. It was clear that we were in for a bad night.

At the end of the road I became aware that I should go and visit an elderly man. I pulled the hand-brake on, leaned back, and sighed. I didn't want to bother. I sat and tried to analyze the feeling and wondered if I was going mad. Perhaps I was just overtired or cornered by guilt, or maybe the Lord was trying to tell me something. This elderly man didn't really need a visit and he wouldn't be expecting me to call on such a snowy afternoon. Several moments passed.

At last I gave in. Instead of turning left toward my home, I turned right toward the man's house. The snow was falling in great white clumps, and the car labored as I drove up the steep hill toward the council estate where he lived.

I went in through the gate and knocked on the back door, as was customary in our mining village. The old man greeted me warmly and put the kettle on. Soon I was

consuming yet another cup of hot strong tea! We chatted
for a while and shared our faith together. The visit ended
with a time of prayer.

I went back home wondering why I'd been to see him.
It made no sense at all! The next morning I learned that
the man had died of a heart attack during the night, and I
had been one of the last people to speak to him. If I
hadn't trusted that feeling and gone to visit him, I think
I'd have lived the rest of my life with a tinge of regret. I'm
sure the Lord guided me because He wanted me to make
that visit that snowy afternoon.

God's call may come at the most inconvenient
moment. It has sometimes overturned my list of priorities,
interrupted my social life and made me late for important
engagements. Sometimes He has overruled what is in my
appointment book and led me into unexpected situations.
His will doesn't always fit neatly around my plans!

Prayer must involve listening. We should listen for the
Lord's voice as we read the Bible or meditate, and be
ready to hear Him at all times and in all situations.

The Lord may want to speak to us while we're at work,
on holiday or, in transit . . . and it may be at a time when
we're not in a "devotional mode"! He may choose to speak
to us in the supermarket, the garage, or the commuter train.

We should be available to hear and to respond, even
in the mundane or the routine. Many of us need to take
the barriers down and become more available. Our work
for Him should become more fully integrated into the
whole of life. Today, open your ears to hear the Lord and
be ready to respond.

Suppose one of you has a servant who comes in from

plowing the field or tending the sheep. Would you take his coat, set the table, and say, "Sit down and eat"? Wouldn't you be more likely to say, "Prepare dinner; change your clothes and wait table for me until I've finished my coffee; then go to the kitchen and have your supper"? Does the servant get special thanks for doing what's expected of him? It's the same with you. When you've done everything expected of you, be matter-of-fact and say, "The work is done. What we were told to do, we did."

Luke 17:7-10

O Thou divine Spirit that,
in all events of life,
art knocking at the door of my heart,

help me to respond to Thee.
I would not be driven blindly as the stars over
        their courses.
I would not be made to work out Thy will
        unwillingly,
to fulfill Thy law unintelligently,
to obey Thy mandates unsympathetically.

I would take the events of my life
as good and perfect gifts from Thee;
I would receive even the sorrows of my life
as disguised gifts from Thee.

I would have my heart open at all times to
        receive—
at morning, noon and night;
in spring, and summer, and winter.

Whether Thou comest to me in sunshine or in
        rain,
I would take Thee into my heart joyfully.
Thou art Thyself more than the sunshine,
Thou art Thyself compensation for the rain;

it is Thee and not Thy gifts I crave;
knock, and I shall open unto Thee.
Amen.

                                    George Matheson

TWENTY

when I can't pray for others

None of us can cope with the suffering of the whole world, nor respond to all of the needs around us, but we all have a God-given commission to care. Many of us need to understand afresh the pain of broken relationships, crushing bereavement, disabling illness and desperate loneliness which overshadows so many lives.

Several years ago I saw the needs of the people around me in a completely new way. I started to write a newspaper agony column which was backed up by a counseling service. The paper was delivered to hundreds of thousands of homes throughout south London, and at one time we had 3,500 "clients" and a staff of ten.

This project opened up a new world of human need to me. I'd been a church minister for nearly ten years, but I'd no idea of the extent of the human suffering all around me. I'd driven around my parish and visited church members, but I'd remained blissfully unaware of the social problems which were present in every street.

At our weekly case conference we came across count-less situations where people had fallen through the net of the caring services. Members of the team found them-selves trying to offer Christian compassion to those facing homelessness, domestic violence, acute depression, and crippling illness.

I had lived in this densely populated community and attended a lively church, yet gone around the area completely unaware of the suffering which lay behind the doors of every street. Many people were fighting for survival in a society that didn't seem to care. I needed to lift my eyes above my own problems to see the dark shadow of suffering on every side.

Jesus was completely immersed in human suffering. His coming demonstrated how sharply the values of His kingdom differed from the values of the world. At His birth He emptied Himself and humbled Himself. He left the riches of heaven for a stable and a homeless family and was made flesh, and in so doing became frail and vulnerable.

During His life he was the "friend of sinners" and shrank from no one. He cared for crooks like Zacchaeus, those of dubious morality like the woman of Samaria, and outcasts like the ten lepers. He became powerless, tasted persecution, and went through torture and humiliation. He became incarnate in human need. He was the Servant King.

One evening at sunset I stood on the Mount of Olives

and looked down at Jerusalem. I remembered the time
when Jesus looked over the same city and wept:
"Jerusalem! Jerusalem! You kill the prophets and stone the
messengers God has sent you! How many times have I
wanted to put my arms round all your people, just as a hen
gathers her chicks under her wings, but you would not let
Me!" (Matt. 23:37).

Jesus had an aching burden for the people of that
great city. He knew their needs and wanted to embrace
them with His love. These were no empty sentiments, but
the expression of One who lived entirely for others. Jesus
loved the world with a depth of compassion that we can't
begin to understand.

Before I pray for others I spend some moments in
silence and try to "feel" the needs of those I'm praying for.
I can only pray effectively if I have a genuine concern.
Too many of us pray from the mind and not from the
heart, and we need to discover a deeper spirit of compassion. We need to learn how to identify with the needs of
those we're praying for.

True intercession transcends words. As we prepare
ourselves to intercede for the world, we need to move
from seeing the suffering around us to actually feeling it.
Only when we "weep with those who weep" are we ready
to intercede for the world.

A prayer of intercession is not made up of meaningless
words. It's a cry from the heart to a loving Father who
moves in ways beyond our understanding. I believe in the
power of prayer and have seen many situations turned
around by the faithful intercessions of God's people. We
should not fill our prayers with "ifs", "buts" or "maybes",
but with a positive faith in a powerful and loving

Heavenly Father. As we cry out to the Lord in prayer we know that Jesus is at the right hand of God interceding for us, and that we have access to the Father through Him.

Today, make sure that your prayer for others is not an escape from responsibility. Prayers for those in need should flow into practical service. And only those who both pray and serve have got the balance right.

So, what do you think? With God on our side like this, how can we lose? If God didn't hesitate to put everything on the line for us, embracing our condition and exposing himself to the worst by sending his own Son, is there anything else he wouldn't gladly and freely do for us? And who would dare tangle with God by messing with one of God's chosen? Who would dare even to point a finger? The One who died for us— who was raised to life for us!—is in the presence of God at this very moment sticking up for us.

Romans 8:31-34

[Picture the faces of those for whom you wish to pray between each phrase]

Dear Father,
I bring before you those who suffer

Whose days are dark
And whose nights are long.

Give them comfort,
Give them peace

And grant them, I pray,
The wonder of Your presence

Right where they are.

TWENTY-ONE

when I'm spiritually low

I meet so many people who say they're suffering from "spiritual lows" and who are looking for something which will give them a more stable prayer life. Over the years, however, I have discovered that the best way to make progress in the life of prayer is to keep on keeping on!

Many Christians who are feeling as though they are in a spiritual wilderness are looking for quick-acting spiritual pick-me-ups, and if they don't find them they quickly become disillusioned. I've found that I'm most likely to rediscover the Lord's blessing and a fresh anointing on my life by just keeping going in the life of prayer.

It is in the plod of Christian fellowship, the plod of a disciplined prayer time, the plod of attendance at worship, and the plod of continuing commitment to Jesus that I discover new blessing.

The Christian plod may not seem very exciting, but I believe that it's the surest way out of the wilderness. It is only as we continue to seek the Lord in prayer through thick and thin that we will find that prayer really works in our lives.

The less we feel like prayer, the more important it is that we pray. It is in the hard work of prayer, the discipline of prayer, the daily plod of prayer, that we give the Lord opportunity to break into our lives and to bring us closer to Him.

At the heart of the "Christian plod" there is a covenant between ourselves and the Lord which is the sure foundation for our faith. It is a covenant which we need to remake and sharpen again and again as the years go by.

In August 1755 John Wesley introduced a simple order of service known as the "Covenant service." It was a powerful time of rededication, and it quickly became a popular event in Methodist fellowships. Methodists all over the world still hold annual Covenant services and they still use the same basic outline prepared by John Wesley.

The Covenant prayer, which is at the heart of the service, takes the "ifs" and "buts" out of Christian commitment and describes explicitly how to live the "Christian plod"! I find this promise harder to make as the years go by. It's not that my commitment to Jesus is any the less, but that the cost of this commitment grows more real as time goes by. Wesley's prayer consists of a number of poignant phrases.

"*I am no longer my own, but yours.*" Only as we resign ourselves completely to His will can we discover His purpose for our lives. In doing so our lives are not something to cling hold of, but something to be given and shared.

"*Put me to what you will, rank me with whom you will.*" Wesley's covenant promise doesn't say, "Put me to what I feel I'm capable of." Even now, after many years in the ministry, I still find myself approaching situations which I don't know how to handle. Sometimes I have stood outside the home of a bereaved family not knowing what to say, or have waited in church vestries feeling inadequate about my preaching. But in submission I have discovered that God could use me, even when my best wasn't good enough.

"*Put me to doing, put me to suffering.*" Whatever God's plan for our lives might involve, we should be ready to accept it and live it for His glory. If our faith collapses when we face suffering, it can't be real. Time and again I've seen Christians use experiences of suffering for the glory of God and, even in the most awful circumstances, find a radiant peace.

"*Let me be employed for you or laid aside for you.*" Active people like myself find these words some of the hardest to say. Many of us who enjoy a hectic lifestyle and ever-changing opportunities for service dread the very thought of stopping! Part of saying "anything" to the Lord is a willingness to be laid aside and a recognition that it's God's work and not our own!

"*Exalted for you or brought low for you.*" Once I came across a sign in a church vestry which read: "You can't convince people that you're a good preacher and that Christ is a wonderful Savior!" It can be difficult to keep walking the path of genuine humility, but in all our work for Him the only thing that really matters is that He is glorified.

"Let me be full, let me be empty; let me have all things, let me have nothing." Whether we own a lot or very little we must realize that we are holding these things "in trust" from Him. When we learn to share what we have and to give to others without holding back, we'll find true joy. Our aim in life shouldn't be to own more, but to share more.

"I freely and wholeheartedly yield all things to your pleasure and disposal." The starting point for all Christian discipleship must be the death of our old selves. The clay must lose its old shape if the Potter is to work with us. If we allow Him to mold our lives we will discover that His will for us is completely perfect.

Today, return to the Christian plod of commitment to Jesus. For in giving yourself to Him you will discover the right way ahead.

Then Jesus went to work on his disciples. "Anyone who intends to come with me has to let me lead. You're not in the driver's seat; I am. Don't run from suffering; embrace it. Follow me and I'll show you how. Self-help is no help at all. Self-sacrifice is the way, my way, to finding yourself, your true self. What kind of deal is it to get everything you want but lose yourself? What could you ever trade your soul for?"

Matthew 16:24-26

I am no longer my own, but yours;
Put me to what you will,
Rank me with whom you will;
Put me to doing,
Put me to suffering;
Let me be employed for you,
Or laid aside for you;
Exalted for you,
Or brought low for you;
Let me be full,
Let me be empty;
Let me have all things,
Let me have nothing;
I freely and wholeheartedly yield
all things to your pleasure
and disposal.

The Covenant Service Prayer,
The Methodist Church

T W E N T Y - T W O

when prayer seems boring

Sometimes I find that I can pray when I'm sitting in an armchair and just chatting things through with the Lord. A cup of coffee, a quiet house and the opportunity of some time without pressing engagements all help to make this time worthwhile. But when I find prayer boring I know that I must vary things to bring a freshness to my devotional life.

The Bible can be a major source of inspiration for prayer. The psalms are like a prayerbook in themselves, and I've often used them to set my mind to praise and worship. "Oh, how grateful and thankful I am to the Lord because he is so good. I will sing praise to the name of the Lord who is above all lords" (Ps. 7:17 TLB).

Sometimes I use hymnbooks to set my heart and mind

along the right track for prayer, and I find their poetry a
powerful form of communication with the Lord.

O Lord my God! when I in awesome wonder
Consider all the worlds Thy hand have made,
I see the stars, I hear the rolling thunder,
Thy power throughout the universe displayed:
Then sings my soul, my Savior God, to Thee,
How great Thou art, how great Thou art!

I also find that liturgical prayer can open the door to a
new world of devotional experience: "God of peace who
brought again from the dead our Lord Jesus Christ, that
great Shepherd of the sheep, by the blood of the eternal
covenant: make us perfect in every good work to do your
will, and work in us that which is well pleasing in your
sight, through Jesus Christ our Lord."

Some of the traditional prayers have a richness
of language which is very stimulating, and their
very familiarity can be a great comfort in times of stress
and strain. "Protect us through the silent hours of this
night, that we who are wearied by the changes and
chances of this fleeting world . . . may rest upon your eternal changelessness." This kind of poetic style is rarely
achieved with extempore prayer when we use the same
phrases ad nauseam until they lose their meaning.

Music is also a helpful accompaniment to prayer.
During difficult times in my life I've attended sung evensong and used the words and music as an inspiration for
devotion. I find that music can lead me to the very throne
of God. I remember an afternoon of prayer over twenty
years ago, guided by the music of Handel's *Messiah*, I used

the words to direct my devotion.

I never understood the importance of art in prayer until I attended a Greek Orthodox cathedral one Sunday morning in Greece. As the worship continued, the people stood up and walked around looking at the icons on the wall. Many of the worshipers paused before these pictures of Jesus as they prayed. Of course we don't worship created objects, but there is no doubt that art can provide a focus for prayer. Sometimes I've used the countryside scenes from calendars as an inspiration for prayer—though a walk in the real countryside is even better!

There is something special about praying in the open air, and I particularly like to pray from a high point over-looking a town. The houses are so small and the community becomes more manageable for prayer! Isaiah glimpsed the Lord's "view of the world" when he wrote: "Do you not know? Were you not told long ago? Have you not heard how the world began? It was made by the One who sits on His throne above the earth and beyond the sky; the people below look as tiny as ants" (Isa. 40:21-22).

In praying over a town we look at the world from the Lord's viewpoint. He sees beyond the ordered streets and deep into the suffering of human hearts, and in praying for a whole community we recognize the Lord's love for each individual within it.

For me the most effective way of praying is to walk. I have a regular route which I try to follow three or four times each week, come rain or shine, and my leisurely stroll down the muddy farm track is like a pilgrimage with the Lord. I have to admit that often I don't feel like going, and that sometimes it's sheer willpower that sets me walking.

It takes me ten minutes to focus on the presence of

the Lord because there's usually a lot of mental junk that I
need to get rid of before I can really praise Him. I enjoy
the familiarity of the route and the scenery. There is a
kind of liturgy in my pilgrimage, as I divide the track into
sections for praise, repentance and prayers for myself.

After twenty minutes I reach a quiet wood and stand
in silence to watch the wildlife and to take in the beauty.
When I turn back toward the car I feel more able to pray
for others, but sometimes the list is so long I have to ask
the Lord to guide me!

Today, seek to begin the changes in your prayer life.
Try something new and be creative and imaginative.
Understand that prayer is a relationship, and while relationships may sometimes be a struggle, they should never
be a bore!

May God, who puts all things together,
  makes all things whole,
Who made a lasting mark through the sacrifice of Jesus,
    the sacrifice of blood that sealed the eternal covenant,
Who led Jesus, our Great Shepherd,
  up and alive from the dead,
Now put you together, provide you
  with everything you need to please him,
Make us into what gives him most pleasure,
    by means of the sacrifice of Jesus, the Messiah.
All glory to Jesus forever and always!
  Oh yes, yes, yes.

                                        Hebrews 13:20-21

Eternal, Holy, Almighty,
whose name is Love,
I come to seek Thy face,
and in spirit and truth to worship Thy name.

I come in deep humility,
since Thou art so high and exalted,
and because Thou beholdest the proud afar off.

I come in tender penitence,
for the contrite heart is Thy only dwelling.

I come in the name and spirit of Jesus
to make my will one with Thine;
to abandon my lonely and selfish walk
for solemn communion with Thee,
to put an end to sin
by welcoming to my heart Thy Holy Presence.

Deeper than I have known,
enter, Thou maker of my soul;
Clearer than I have ever seen,
dawn Thy glory on my sight.

Light the flame upon the altar,
Call forth the incense of prayer,
Waken the song of praise,
and manifest Thyself to all.
Amen.

                                        W. E. Orchard

TWENTY-THREE

when I'm angry with God

Life isn't easy, and there have been many times when I've felt confused about things and even been angry with God. I once went through a difficult time of questioning when I was a young minister in Yorkshire.

I was taking a young family to a hospital near Leeds. In the back of the car, huddled in a blanket, was a little three-year-old boy. This child had been a bundle of energy just a few months before, but had grown weak and frail because he was crippled with cancer.

I watched his pale drawn face in my rearview mirror as we drove the weary miles to the special pediatric cancer unit. His parents knew that the chemotherapy treatment was putting an enormous strain on him. They didn't know where to turn in their distress.

As we waited outside the treatment room we sat in stony silence. His father walked up the corridor and back, sat down for a while, then walked off again. No words could console him. We watched people come and go, and time stood still.

There were no texts to quote. No theological statements to make. Every argument I knew about "the problem of pain" was silenced. I had nothing to say.

For days afterwards my mind was in turmoil. I asked the Lord to show me why this child had to suffer; but there was no reply, just a hollow emptiness. The question of suffering hung heavy on my mind.

There have been times like this when I have been unspeakably angry with God, and there have been times when prayer has been suffocated by doubt. Sometimes pastoral situations have been so bleak that God has seemed completely out of touch.

I haven't suppressed these feelings and I've tried to bring them into the arena of my relationship with God. Over the years only one image has helped me through these times of questioning: a mental picture of Jesus on the cross—and the words of dereliction, "My God, my God, why have you forsaken me?" (Matt. 28:46 TLB).

In my heart, I know that Jesus understands about suffering, and that He really does care. The fact that Jesus lives on the inside of suffering was brought home to me during a hospital visit near my home.

My visit to the hospital in the center of Croydon was an unusual one. I was visiting an older minister suffering from a rare blood disease. The prognosis wasn't good. As I entered the dull Victorian ward he shouted a friendly greeting and shuffled toward me in a bright silk dressing gown. He was very glad to see me, and I him.

You can't do a "professional" visit with a fellow minister. They know the catchphrases and see past the courtesies. You can talk frankly without the formalities. This minister told me that his time of illness had been a time of learning, and there was a lot that he wanted to share.

"In all my years as a hospital chaplain," he confided, "I never realized what it was like to be stuck in here. I used to breeze in and out and say nice things to people, but I was always on the outside looking in. But now, you see, I'm on the inside too. I get woken up at some ungodly hour. I suffer those wretched transfusions every day. I don't know what the future holds—I'm going through the mill like everyone else. Because of that the other patients let me get close to them, and let me pray with them. I've done more as a patient here in a few weeks than in years of hospital chaplaincy."

He saw his time in the hospital as a parable of the Incarnation, for Jesus lives on the inside of suffering too. David Shepherd wrote: "The incarnation meant truly entering into a world where there was indignation, corrupt authority, sickness, adultery, betrayal, agony and bloody sweat. If we believe that God is really incarnate, He is frighteningly close; He meets us where we are."

Questioning the Lord is a much neglected aspect of prayer. The book of Job is a demonstration of how that kind of prayer is part of a living relationship with the Lord. Blind faith and suppressed feelings do not make for a real relationship of any kind and they certainly don't help us to be real with our Heavenly Father. Job said:

I still rebel and complain against God; I can't hold back my groaning. How I wish I knew where to find

him, and knew how to go where he is. I would state
my case before him and present all the arguments in
my favor. I want to know what he would say and how
he would answer me. Would God use all his strength
against me? No, he would listen as I spoke. I am
honest; I could reason with God; he would declare me
innocent once and for all (Job 23:1-7).

Today, don't be afraid of bringing your deepest hurts,
sorrows and questions to the Lord. Part of prayer is letting
go of the anger that wells up within you. For, even when
you can't find answers to your questions, you need to
know that God is with you in the confusion.

*God means what he says. What he says goes. His power-
ful Word is sharp as a surgeon's scalpel, cutting through
everything, whether doubt or defense, laying us open to listen
and obey. Nothing and no one is impervious to God's Word.
We can't get away from it—no matter what.*

*Now that we know what we have—Jesus, this great High
Priest with ready access to God—let's not let it slip through our
fingers. We don't have a priest who is out of touch with our
reality. He's been through weakness and testing, experienced it
all—all but the sin. So let's walk right up to him and get what
he is so ready to give. Take the mercy, accept the help.*

Hebrews 4:12-16

The nurse went up a flight of stairs,
The hallway rang with noise.
The smell of disinfectant filled the air,
I turned into the ward—
And looked along the row of beds,
And saw the face I knew.

The eyes were different now,
Sullen,
Sad,
And dry.
I could not speak.
No word was adequate.

I went and took the thin white hand in mine,
And touched the agony.
A jarring shock ran through my soul,
And time stood still.

I shrank away defeated
Asking . . . why?
I cannot understand.

A picture fills my mind.
A vivid picture of a bloodstained cross.
A voice cries out through time . . .
My God . . . My God . . . why?
Lord Jesus, You have gone before,
Give me Your strength . . .
To shout through my confusion . . .
Thy will be done.

TWENTY-FOUR

when I can't see results

One summer I went to help my friend bring in the harvest on his Yorkshire farm. I had no idea what harvesting would be like, but as I learned how to drive the tractor, throw bales of straw into the barn, and unclog the bailer, I began to realize just how stressful an occupation farming can be! Each night my friend and I would stagger back into the farmhouse covered in grime, but with a glow of satisfaction that "all was safely gathered in." Harvesting is hard work!

Many Christians feel that the area where they are "gathering the harvest of the kingdom" is particularly difficult. Those working in suburbia talk of apathy and materialism; those working in villages bemoan traditionalism and the occult; and those working in the inner city point to problems created by acute social need. Many Christians feel that it must be easier to witness for the Lord somewhere else.

In Christian ministry the grass may seem greener on the other side of the hill, but if the truth was known, those fields may be just as hard to work in! The history of mission demonstrates that the hardest ground can sometimes yield the best crop when it has been prayed over consistently.

A few years ago I met a young Indian Christian called Augustine. He'd had a dream in which the Lord called him to give up everything and go to northern India to plant new churches. In simple obedience he sold his home, left his job, and moved with his family to northern India.

He couldn't interest any missionary society in his vision, but two elderly Elim missionaries in the region decided to support him. They had worked and prayed there for many years, but had found the people hard and unresponsive.

They welcomed Augustine's family into their home and encouraged them in the early days of their ministry. Soon their term of service was over and they came back to England. It was a sad departure because their faithful work over many years had evoked such little response.

Augustine took on the work and eventually he led some hardened criminals in the local prison to faith in Christ. These conversions had such an effect on the local community that a church was formed.

Later, Augustine recruited others from the congregation to join him as evangelists, and soon they were planting congregations in many of the villages around the area. There was still great opposition, but many came to know Christ as Savior.

I saw Augustine make a historic speech at the annual
Elim conference. He paid tribute to the prayers of those
two elderly ladies and admitted that they had prepared the
ground for the harvest. At this conference meeting
Augustine named a score of new churches "Elim" in recognition of the faithfulness of these pioneer missionaries.

Much of our thinking in the church focuses on what
we can do and what our planning and effort can achieve,
but the history of the church demonstrates again and
again that where God's people pray faithfully, there grows
a mighty harvest.

I am convinced that where there is faithful prayer the
harvest follows. Much of the work of evangelism is done
in prayer, and unless the ground is drenched with the
prayers of the faithful it will remain hard and barren.

Today, pray for those involved in the mission of the
church. Pray for areas unreached by the Gospel. Pray for
people who don't know Christ as Lord. Prepare the
ground for a mighty harvest.

*Jesus was matter-of-fact: "Embrace this God-life. Really
embrace it, and nothing will be too much for you. This moun-
tain, for instance: Just say, 'Go jump in the lake'—no
shuffling or shilly-shallying—and it's as good as done. That's
why I urge you to pray for absolutely everything, ranging from
small to large. Include everything as you embrace this God-
life, and you'll get God's everything."*
Mark 11:22-24

O great Lord of the harvest, send forth, we
    beseech Thee,
laborers into the harvest of the world,
that the grain which is even now ripe may not
    fall and perish through our neglect.
Pour forth Thy sanctifying Spirit on our
    fellow Christians abroad,
and Thy converting grace on those who are
    living in darkness.
Raise up, we beseech Thee, a devout
    ministry, that,
all Thy people being knit together in one
    body, love,
Thy church may grow up into the measure of
    the stature of the fullness of Christ;
through Him who died, and rose again for us
    all,
the same Jesus Christ our Lord.
Amen.

Bishop Milman (1791-1868)

TWENTY-FIVE

when I stand alone

Christian discipleship can be difficult whatever your age, and the society in which we live can sometimes seem very unsympathetic. Those of us who are committed to the Lord face many different pressures as we serve Christ and try to live lives worthy of our calling.

If you actively seek to win others for Christ you may well become the butt of humor. Go "public" about your faith, make a stand on some ethical issue, say "no" to back-handers, tell the truth—and people will probably oppose you.

Read the Bible on the train, speak about Jesus in the staffroom, invite friends to church—and you'll sense just how much you differ from the crowd! Anyone who stands up for Jesus may find themselves standing on their own.

Paul knew the pain of this kind of isolation. In Corinth he was working among the Jewish community and testified that Jesus was the Messiah. But "they opposed him and said evil things about him" (Acts 18:6). It must have been hard for him to be rejected by his own people and to know the pain of lonely isolation.

In his isolation he had a beautiful vision of Jesus. The Lord said, "Do not be afraid, but keep on speaking and do not give up, for I am with you." When Paul felt as though everyone else had rejected him, he discovered that Jesus was still there.

The Christian life is often difficult, and the journey of discipleship may take us through times when we feel we're standing completely alone. When we face trouble, opposition and suffering, He may not take us out of the situation, but if we ask, He will provide the strengthening comfort of His presence.

When Hudson Taylor was onboard the old steamship *Lammermuir* bound for China, he felt both physically and emotionally at the end. The boat went through a terrible storm, and for sixteen days the wind and waves pounded the little vessel. The passengers and crew prepared to die.

At this all-time low Taylor wrote:

Burdens, such as I never before sustained,
Responsibilities such as I had not hitherto incurred,
And sorrows—compared with which all my past
sorrows were light, have been part of my experience . . .
But I trust I have in some feeble measure learned more
of the blessed truth that—"sufficient is His arm alone
and our defense is sure."

I often ponder the words "I am the bread of life. He who comes to me will never go hungry" (John 6:35 NIV) when I distribute bread at the Eucharist. I look at the different hands outstretched to receive and I am often moved. Black hands and white hands; some wrinkled with age, others young and smooth. Hands gnarled by work. Hands twisted with arthritis. Hands open to receive. The hands of people who are passing through days of loneliness and hardship.

As I place bread in each hand I am symbolizing that Christ's presence will be bread for the coming days. And as these folk rise from the Lord's Table, they are going out in the strength of the Bread of Life. He alone can give the grace sufficient for every need.

Sometimes I would have liked the Lord to change things overnight or to take me away from difficult situations, but it hasn't happened. The next day the situation is the same, the problem hasn't changed, and the difficult relationships are still to be faced. And yet, somehow, everything is different. Through the strengthening power of Jesus, I've been changed, I've been strengthened, I've been renewed. I've discovered the empowering presence of Christ with me in the situation.

Today, if you feel that the isolation of your situation is too great to bear, it is time to receive the Bread of Life. It is at your weakest point, when no one seems near, that you can find strength for the journey ahead through Christ, the Bread of Life.

I've learned by now to be quite content whatever my circumstances. I'm just as happy with little as with much, with much as with little. I've found the recipe for being happy whether full or hungry, hands full or hands empty. Whatever I have, wherever I am, I can make it through anything in the One who makes me who I am.

Philippians 4:11-13

The Bread of Life

In a village a boy stood watching
A baker baking bread
He watched the kneading of the dough
And the shaping into loaves
He felt the heat of the oven's fire
He smelt that baking smell
And when they asked him what he'd do
I'll feed them bread, he said.

A man stood and watched crowds walk away
Taking in lessons learned
His friends gathered left-over food
from a meal they all had shared
And twelve baskets full of barley loaves
Was what there was to spare
For when they'd asked him what he'd do
I'll feed them bread, he said.

When the people asked him for a sign
Food sent down from heaven
The truth is I'm the bread of life
And although you don't believe
If it's life that you are seeking, then
Of me you'll have to eat
I am the bread the Father sent
I'll feed you bread, he said.

This can't be true, in anger they cried
How can we eat your flesh?
Unless you do, he told them all

And also drink of my blood
Then within you there cannot be life.
I give that the world might live
And when you ask me who I am
I'll feed you bread, he said.

And at a table sat the man with
A number of his friends
Taking a loaf, breaking it said
This is my body broken
And the wine in this cup is my blood
Poured out in forgiveness
Eat, drink, so you'll never forget
I'm feeding you bread, he said.

As night fell on the Emmaus Road
We ate with a stranger
Who'd shared with us from scripture
and then taken up a loaf
I recognized him as he blessed it
And breaking it, shared it
His body that's broken for me
I'm feeding you bread, he said,
I'm feeding you bread, he said.

Steve Deal, from Breaking Bread

TWENTY - SIX

when I've lost sight of Jesus

I find that prayer is often a struggle. There always seems
to be a hundred and one distractions and seemingly more
urgent things to do.

I know, however, that if I neglect my relationship with
Jesus my Christian life will just wither and die. Prayer is
something I'm always trying to tackle in different ways.

Prayerwalking is my favorite kind of praying, but there
are other locations that sometimes help. My study is
sometimes the setting for the work of intercession.
Sometimes I make a list of those in special need and work
through it name by name.

The local library is my venue for reflection and meditation. I withdraw into the silence of the study area with
my Bible, and ask God to speak to me. Time and again

the words have leaped out in relevance to my own situation and need.

Sometimes in the dense London traffic I turn off the car radio and have a chat with the Lord about the events of the day. Even there, in the frustration of rush hour, I've known the Lord's presence in a powerful way.

Quite often in counseling situations, committees or worship services I'm silently talking to the Lord about the situations I'm facing. Where appropriate I try to pray with people when they visit me, and frequently pray with people over the phone.

But Jesus is at the center of the life of prayer. Without Him it's all pointless, for He is the One who hears and who intercedes. Time and again I've had to discover a fresh love for Him.

Napoleon said, "I know men, and there is no term of comparison between Jesus and any other man who ever lived." Jesus was unique and different. Truly God, yet truly man.

Peter wrote, "We have not depended on made-up legends in making known to you the mighty coming of our Lord Jesus Christ. With our own eyes we saw His greatness. We were there when He was given honor and glory by the Father" (2 Peter 1:16-17).

Historian Sir James Frazer said that "the doubts which have been cast on the historical reality of Jesus are, in my judgment, unworthy of serious attention."

J. N. Geldenhuys explained that "the whole course of world history during the last nineteen hundred years is inexplicable apart from the historical fact that Jesus Christ lived, died, and rose again."

William Lecky noted that "those three short years of

active life have done more to regenerate and soften mankind than all the disquisitions of philosophers and the exhortations of moralists."

Oxford don C.S. Lewis declared: "Either this man was the Son of God—or He was a madman or something worse," and when Swiss theologian Karl Barth was asked about his most profound concept in Christianity he replied, "Jesus loves me, this I know, for the Bible tells me so."

James Irwin, the astronaut who walked on the moon, said, "It is more significant that God walked on earth than that man walked on the moon." Canon Michael Green said, "All other great teachers said, 'Follow that,' but he claimed to be the truth and said, 'Follow me.'"

Cliff Richard wrote, "If this love is true—then it has to be the most radical, urgent, and relevant piece of Good News ever to be delivered. Personally I am as convinced about the truth of it as I am about anything."

Celia Haddon, editor of *The Sunday Times Book of Body Maintenance*, stated, "I needed, desperately needed, some help and comfort in my attempt to lead a good life. Christ offered that support."

Jesus is the One to whom we may pray, and in whose presence the life of prayer is nourished. See Him gathering the children around Himself, setting them on His knee and blessing them. Know again how much He cared for every one of them, and how He cares for you.

See Him reaching out to the untouchables. See Him caring for the despised and the broken people with no hope and no future. Watch Him with the outcasts, the losers, the drop-outs, and the poor who are trapped in a downward spiral of decline. Sense His quality of compassion. See Him making them whole, and know that He can do the same for you.

See the Lord raising up the paralyzed man—and helping him to hobble those first halting steps. Hear His words of forgiveness and His promise of healing. Glimpse Him breaking the bread and pouring the wine, and hear His promise of a new kingdom.

See Him hanging crucified. Hear Him declare, "Father, forgive them." See Him standing beside Galilee and forgiving Peter, the one who let Him down.

Today, know that He is with you. Understand that He has loved you since before you knew His name. Know that He's been beside you through the good and the bad. Remember that, in His love, you can find full salvation, the purpose of your being.

I am the Gate. Anyone who goes through me will be cared for—will freely go in and out, and find pasture. A thief is only there to steal and kill and destroy. I came so they can have real and eternal life, more and better life than they ever dreamed of.

I am the Good Shepherd. The Good Shepherd puts the sheep before himself, sacrifices himself if necessary. A hired man is not a real shepherd. The sheep mean nothing to him. He sees a wolf come and runs for it, leaving the sheep to be ravaged and scattered by the wolf. He's only in it for the money. The sheep don't matter to him.

I am the Good Shepherd. I know my own sheep and my own sheep know me.

John 10:9-14

Freedom from fear
is knowing who controls tomorrow.

Freedom from failure
is knowing who gives new beginnings.

Freedom from insecurity
is knowing who always stays the same.

Freedom from guilt
is knowing who paid the price of forgiveness.

Freedom from sin
is knowing who is bigger than temptation.

Freedom from worry
is knowing who has all the answers.

Freedom from hang-ups
is knowing who can let the real me out.

Freedom to become
The person Jesus intended me to be.

TWENTY - SEVEN

when I'm
under attack

The older I get, the more convinced I become that there is an active power of evil in the world. The old-fashioned images of a sooty-faced creature with horns don't have any credibility with me . . . the Devil is far more sophisticated than that!

I've discovered that an important part of personal prayer discipline is to seek to overcome the Devil and all his ways through the power of the Lord. Peter wrote: "Be alert, be on the watch! Your enemy, the Devil, roams around like a roaring lion, looking for someone to devour. Be firm in your faith and resist him" (1 Peter 5:8-9).

Sometimes in church life things seem to be falling apart! Over the years I've come to look behind the division, the discord or the lack of discipline to ask, "Who's behind all this . . . and why?" Often, I've sensed that these are the works of the Evil One being presented in human situations.

Paul wrote: "For we are not fighting against human beings but against the wicked spiritual forces in the heavenly world, the rulers, authorities, and cosmic powers of this dark age" (Eph. 6:12). Spiritual warfare is an important everyday aspect of the life of prayer.

In the old pagan festival of Samhain, the forerunner of Halloween, people lit bonfires to give light, they threw nuts into them to make noise, they disguised themselves with soot and put evil-faced pumpkins around the village to ward off spirits. They did these things because they were afraid of the Devil, and scared of what he might do to them.

As Christians, however, we have no need to fear him, for Paul wrote: "And on that cross Christ freed himself from the power of the spiritual rulers and authorities; he made a public spectacle of them by leading them as captives in his victory procession" (Col. 2:15).

When we take authority over the Evil One we need not be afraid. Our old lives are buried with Christ, and we've been raised to live a new life by His mighty power. We are "in Christ", and the power within us is greater than the power that is in the world!

When the seventy-two disciples returned to Jesus rejoicing that the demons had obeyed them, Jesus replied: "Listen! I have given you authority, so that you can walk on snakes and scorpions and overcome all the power of the Enemy, and nothing will hurt you. But don't be glad because the evil spirits obey you; rather be glad because your names are written in heaven" (Luke 10:19-20). We have the authority, in Christ, to dismiss the legions of the Enemy!

Several years ago I was on a mission in Cyprus, and one afternoon I had the opportunity to go to the town of Paphos. The Roman governor Sergius Paulus used to live there many centuries ago. It was a great thrill to stand in the archaeological dig on the site of his palace and see the beautiful mosaics in his reception hall. This was the very place where he would have interviewed Saul and Barnabas during their mission on the island.

Paul's witness to the governor was a strategic part of his mission, but an evil magician called Bar-Jesus disrupted this work at every turn. Finally Paul took authority over this man's evil ways and declared, "You son of the devil—you are the enemy of everything that's good." A thick mist came over the magician's eyes, and, as a result, Sergius was won for Christ. If Paul had not confronted the works of the Enemy, his mission would have been thwarted.

I am happy to say that I'm not one of those Christians who sees demons around every corner or who lives in a daily paranoia about the works of the Evil One. I do believe, however, that Satan wants to confuse us and derail us, and that if we're living our lives in the power of the risen Jesus Christ he doesn't stand a chance!

Burglaries are fairly common where I live in southwest London, but thankfully armed robberies are still relatively uncommon. Recently, two men armed with automatic handguns attacked our local sub-post office. Bullets hit the door, shelves, and walls . . . but mercifully no one was injured. One customer, so outraged by what he saw, told the men off and chased them down the street! They got away with nothing.

This news story is a parable of how we should face up to the Devil. He seems menacing, threatening, and dangerous, but when we order him away in the name and power of Jesus he turns and runs! James wrote: "Resist the Devil, and he will run away from you" (4:7).

Sometimes in my prayerwalks I have had to take authority over the Evil One in my inner life, and sometimes I've had to ask him to get out of some aspect of my mission or ministry. The life of prayer is a particular target for his activity because when he stops me from praying he stops me from being effective.

Sometimes we can feel trapped by the works of the Evil One. He can entwine himself around our lives and the things we do with great cunning and effectiveness. We must ask Jesus to disentangle us from the Devil and all his ways. We need to discover that in Jesus there is always a way of escape.

Today, ask the Lord to reveal the ways in which the Enemy is active in your life. Take authority over the Evil One. Jesus has risen victorious from the dead. Satan is defeated. You already have the victory—it's yours to claim. Don't just believe it—live in it too!

Don't be so naive and self-confident. You're not exempt. You could fall flat on your face as easily as anyone else. Forget about self-confidence; it's useless. Cultivate God-confidence.

No test or temptation that comes your way is beyond the course of what others have had to face. All you need to remember is that God will never let you down; he'll never let you be pushed past your limit; he'll always be there to help you come through it.

1 Corinthians 10:12-13

Strong Son of God,
who was tried and tested to the uttermost,
yet without sin;
be near me now with Thy strength
and give me victory over the evil desires
that threaten to ruin me.

I am weak, O Lord, and full of doubts and
    fears.
There are moments when I am afraid of myself,
when the world and the flesh and the devil
seem more powerful than the forces of good.

But now I look to Thee
in whom dwelleth
all the fullness of grace
            and might
            and redemption.

Blessed Savior!
I take Thee afresh to be my Refuge,
                my Cover,
                my Defense,
                my strong Tower
                from the enemy.

Hear me and bless me
now and ever.
Amen.

                        Samuel M'Comb

TWENTY-EIGHT

when things aren't working out

One day I was asked to visit a Christian lady who was going through a time of deep depression. Her husband showed me into the darkened bedroom where she lay looking up at the ceiling. I sat on the bed beside her and read from my little pocket Bible about the end times, when pain, suffering, and death will be no more. It was my "prescription" for her situation.

As I read, I sensed her despair beginning to lift and she started to see that there was hope for the future. Months later she told me that this conversation had been a turning point in her recovery. The glimpse of the New City had given her strength to face the present.

Cardinal Basil Hume wrote:

Everything that is in me cries out for the need to reach a destination where there will be no more tears or pain, and where all my deepest aspirations and desires will be finally and completely satisfied. The thought of arriving at the place where all these things will be, and the thought of someone who will put it all right, that can keep me going. Every pilgrim cheerfully puts up with the journey when the going is rough, precisely because there is something to look forward to at the end of it.

Jesus promised that He would prepare a place for us, and this promise has been a source of hope and strength for Christians over many centuries. When we accept that all things really are working together for good, we can see a glimmer of light, even in the darkest hour.

Isaiah was writing from a situation which seemed completely hopeless. He was a prisoner in Babylon, Israel had fallen and the temple was destroyed. He was surrounded by people who could see no hope and no future. It was into this despair that he spoke his vision. He saw beyond the grief and dereliction of the Exile, to the time when the watchmen on the city walls would see messengers coming over the horizon.

He could even hear their message! The Babylonian empire had fallen, and the people of Israel were free again! The messengers were declaring, "Our God reigns!" The Israelites could go back home!

"Hark," Isaiah wrote, "your watchmen lift up their voice, together they sing for joy; for eye to eye they see the return of the Lord to Zion" (Isa. 52:8).

His vision must have seemed like a fantasy. There was

no evidence for such a possibility. There were no messengers, and no watchmen shouting for joy. They were living in dark days.

But in the fullness of time Isaiah's vision was realized—his prophecy was fulfilled. The messengers did appear, and the wonderful news was proclaimed. At last the Israelites went home. At a time of dark hopelessness and despair Isaiah had glimpsed God's perspective. He saw a vision of the future which could bring strength and hope in the midst of trouble.

Scholars tell us that Isaiah's prophecy was a parable of an even greater victory. He could see beyond the struggles of his own time to the Lord's ultimate victory when evil would be removed forever. Isaiah declared God's promise: "I am making a new earth and new heavens. The events of the past will be completely forgotten" (Isa. 65:17). It was a vision of God's eternal kingdom.

One of the most difficult night watches I ever shared also turned out to be one of the most beautiful. I was left in a darkened bedroom with a man who was desperately ill and I was aware that he would not see morning. He drifted from lucidity to coma. When he was able to talk he spoke with a perspective which only death can bring. As he reflected on his life and his career he concluded that only three things held any significance. His faith, his family, and his friends.

As our conversation drew toward its end I told him the wonderful story of Pilgrim's Progress, and shared the beautiful description of Pilgrim's journey across the river of death.

Now I further saw that between them and the gate was a river, but there was no bridge to go over, and

the river was very deep. At the sight, therefore, of this
river the pilgrims were much stunned; but the man
that went with them said, "You must go through, or
you cannot come in at the gate . . ."

Then they addressed themselves to the water and
entering, Christian began to sink; and crying out to
his good friend Hopeful, he said, "I sink in deep
waters; the billows go over my head; all his waves go
over me."

Then I saw in my dream that Christian was in a
muse a while. To whom also Hopeful added this
word—"Be of good cheer, Jesus Christ maketh thee
whole." And with that Christian brake out with a
loud voice, "Oh, I see Him again! and He tells me,
'When thou passest through the waters, I will be with
thee; and through the rivers, they shall not overflow
thee.'" Then they both took courage, and the enemy
was, after that, as still as a stone, until they were gone
over.

Shortly after I had shared this wonderful story with my
friend he passed away, and a beautiful stillness descended
on the room. He had crossed the river to the further shore.

Today, put prayer into God's perspective. Recognize
that even if you feel as though you're sinking in deep
waters, and that the waves may be over your head, He is
still with you. By His strength alone you will yet reach the
place called Paradise on the further shore.

*I saw Heaven and earth new-created. Gone the first
Heaven, gone the first earth, gone the sea.*

I saw Holy Jerusalem, new-created, descending resplendent out of Heaven, as ready for God as a bride for her husband.
I heard a voice thunder from the Throne: "Look! Look! God has moved into the neighborhood, making his home with men and women! They're his people, he's their God. He'll wipe every tear from their eyes. Death is gone for good—tears gone, crying gone, pain gone—all the first order of things gone." The Enthroned continued, "Look! I'm making everything new. Write it all down—each word dependable and accurate."

Revelation 21:1-5

I asked the Lord that I might grow
In faith, and love, and every grace,
Might more of His salvation know
And seek more earnestly His face.

'Twas He who taught me thus to pray
And He, I trust, has answered prayer;
But it has been in such a way
As almost drove me to despair.

I hoped that in some favored hour
At once He'd answer my request,
and by His love's constraining power
Subdue my sins, and give me rest.

Instead of this, He made me feel
The hidden evil of my heart,
and let the angry powers of hell
Assault my soul in every part.

Yea, more, with His own hand He seemed
Intent to aggravate my woe,
Crossed all the fair designs I schemed,
Blasted my gourds, and laid me low.

"Lord, why is this?" I trembling cried,
"Wilt Thou pursue Thy worm to death?"
"'Tis in this way," the Lord replied,
"I answer prayer for grace and faith.

"These inward trials I employ
From self and pride to set thee free,
And break thy schemes of earthly joy,
That thou mayest seek thy all in Me."

John Newton

If you liked this book,
   check out these great titles from
       Chariot Victor Publishing . . .

The Reflective Life
by Ken Gire
ISBN 1-56476-726-4

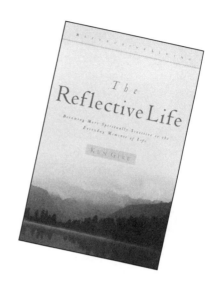

Written by thought-provoking author Ken Gire, this book
is the cornerstone of the "Reflective Living Series." It
introduces readers to three habits that nurture a reflective
life–reading, reflection, and response–and helps them apply
these habits to their lives.

Ken Gire is the author of more than a dozen books, including
Intimate Moments with the Savior, Windows of the Soul,
and Between Heaven and Earth. *He is a graduate of Texas
Christian University and Dallas Theological Seminary and
formerly served as Director of Educational Products at
Insight for Living. Ken and his family live in Colorado.*

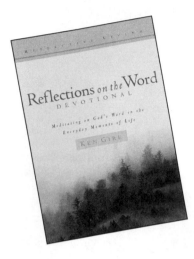

Reflections on the Word
Devotional
by Ken Gire
ISBN: 1-56476-751-5

Designed to help readers develop the habit of slow-
ing down to digest God's Word, this book features
selected Scripture passages—as well as reflections and
prayers not only from the author but from believers
around the world and across the centuries.

Reflections on Your
Life Journal
by Ken Gire
ISBN 1-56476-725-6

This journal helps readers apply the lifestyle
described in *The Reflective Life* by recording what
God is teaching them. Space is provided to record
observations, prayers, and personal applications.

Pause for Power
by Warren Wiersbe
ISBN: 1-56476-757-4

Penned by Warren Wiersbe, one of the most beloved Bible teachers of our time, this spiritually nuturing 12-month devotional delves into a dozen different books of the Bible—Job, Ecclesiates and Isaiah in the Old Testament and Colossians, Romans, 1-2 Corinthians, Hebrews, 1 Peter, Philippians, James, and I John in the New Testament. It offers nuggets of biblical wisdom to encourage and inspire readers in their daily walk, and in the process explores 12 Christian character qualities, including contentment, hope, patience, joy, and comfort.

Dr. Wiersbe is Writer-in-Residence at Cornerstone College in Grand Rapids, Michigan, and Distinguished Professor of Preaching at Grand Rapids Baptist Seminary. He has pastored three churches, including Moody Church in Chicago, and served as General Director and Bible teacher for Back to the Bible Broadcast.